TOUGH BREAKS

THE STORY OF

BALTIMORE CLUB MUSIC

TOUGH BREAKS

THE STORY OF

BALTIMORE CLUB MUSIC

Al Shipley

Published by Repeater Books

An imprint of Watkins Media Ltd

Unit 11 Shepperton House

89-93 Shepperton Road

London

N1 3DF

United Kingdom

www.repeaterbooks.com

A Repeater Books paperback original 2025

1

Distributed in the United States by Random House, Inc., New York.

ISBN: 9781917516068

Ebook ISBN: 9781917516075

Printed and bound by CPI Group (UK) Ltd, Croydon, CR0 4YY

The manufacturer's authorised representative in the EU for product safety is:
eucomply OÜ - Pärnu mnt 139b-14, 11317 Tallinn, Estonia, hello@eucompliancepartner.com, www.eucompliancepartner.com

MIX
Paper | Supporting
responsible forestry
FSC® C013604

Table of Contents

Acknowledgments

My path toward writing this book began almost exactly 20 years ago, when I received an email from Bret McCabe in the spring of 2005. I was finishing up my undergrad degree in English at Towson University, but I hadn't actually planned on a career in writing at that point, or had any plan at all, really. I'd taken up writing about my favorite subject, music, but only as a hobby. I had written a couple dozen album reviews for *Pitchfork*, years before they started paying writers. I'd started a hip hop blog, *Government Names*, with Dylan King, a brilliant and weird young Canadian guy with a comprehensive knowledge of Houston hip hop, and I started using the site as a vehicle to write about Baltimore rap and a local style of dance music called Baltimore club music.

After I wrote a 1,700-word *Government Names* post about Baltimore rapper Tim Trees and his work with club music producer Rod Lee, Bret reached out to me about writing for the *Baltimore City Paper*, where he was music editor. I'd grown up reading my father's issues of the local alternative weekly paper cover to cover, and it was one of the great thrills of my life to start contributing to *City Paper* and working with Bret, editor in chief Lee Gardner, and other people I'd been reading for years. A $35 check for a Will Smith album review was the first money I ever made writing, and over the next couple years Bret allowed me lots of opportunities to grow my confidence and abilities in covering the Baltimore scene and interviewing the artists in the city that I was interested in.

Bret had the initial idea for a *City Paper* oral history of Baltimore club music, and asked me to collaborate with him on the piece. In the summer of 2006, I wrote a piece about the cross pollination between club music and hip hop, and spoke to producers including DJ Booman, Dukeyman, Debonair Samir, Blaqstarr, and Say Wut. In 2007, *City Paper* started publishing online-exclusive content that wouldn't appear in the print edition, and Lee asked me to take a major role in the site's music blog, *Noise*. I used it as an opportunity to delve deeper into the Baltimore club scene, and created a monthly column, The Club Beat, named in homage to Kelly Connelly's Street Beat column in another local paper, *Music Monthly*.

The Club Beat ran through 2011, and as I interviewed dozens of Baltimore club DJs and producers, I'd periodically send my interview transcripts to Bret so we could accumulate material for our big project. Eventually, though, Bret moved to the arts editor's desk, admitted that he didn't think he was going to get around to the Baltimore club history piece, and encouraged me to do it myself. I continued building up my archive of interviews and covering Baltimore music under other *City Paper* editors like Jess Harvell, Michael Byrne, Evan Serpick, and Brandon Soderberg, and alongside a lot of writers I have enormous respect for, including Jason Torres, Tom Breihan, Jay Hunnie, Lawrence Burney, and Baynard Woods. I also had opportunities to write for the daily paper, the *Baltimore Sun*, thanks to Sam Sessa.

Around 2010, I started to feel like there were so many stories and personalities in Baltimore club, so much musical history and creativity in the scene, that it would make more sense as a book than even a very long article. I came up with the title *Tough Breaks*, and asked for and received Bret's blessing to turn his initial idea into something bigger. I announced to the world that I was going to write this book and raised a small amount of money, really far too little money, on the then-new fundraising platform Kickstarter to self-publish it. I received some very generous donations and other kinds of help, like my old friend Josh Dowling creating a mockup book cover for the Kickstarter, and Lawrence Lanahan getting me on the air on WYPR to talk about the project.

As you can surmise from the fact that you're only now holding the book in your hands 15 years later, I did not follow through on my initial 2010 plan to write and publish *Tough Breaks* in a much shorter amount of time. I was a new father, I was changing careers, and it just became easier to meet all my freelancing deadlines and keep delaying finishing the book than to focus on the book and not have as much freelancing income. I know this book could've been finished a long time ago, and I have a little regret about jumping the gun on the Kickstarter. But I lost my nerve for doing it all myself, and the opportunity to publish it with Repeater Books was what I needed to finally get it done. I'm very appreciative to Repeater's Tariq Goddard for taking on this project, and to my patient and insightful editor Carl Neville. If I'm ever in London or if Carl's ever in America, I hope we can meet up and grab a beer.

The worst part about taking so many years to complete a project like this is that a few people who supported it early on are not alive today to see it. My father, Richard Shipley, who died in 2017, was always an enormous influence on me, and fostered both my love of writing and my love of Baltimore. Over the years he dabbled in writing a novel or a children's book or a memoir, and I know he was proud of my decision to become an author. A couple of the Baltimore club greats I interviewed, Jimmy Jones and Ron "Dukeyman" Hall, passed away far too soon, in 2021 and 2024, respectively. Dwayne Lawson, a Baltimore hip hop producer I knew and had great respect for, who donated to the Kickstarter, also died in 2021.

Baltimore City Paper also did not survive the lengthy gestation of this book. In 2014, it was sold to the *Baltimore Sun*'s parent company, Tribune Publishing, who ceased publishing *City Paper* in 2017. *City Paper*'s online archives, including hundreds of articles I wrote, were moved, partially and poorly, to the *Sun*'s website. David D. Smith, the right wing idealogue whose Sinclair Broadcast Group has turned the local news on hundreds of TV stations across America into a bullhorn for conservative talking points and disinformation, acquired a majority ownership of the *Baltimore Sun* in 2024. *The Sun* was a great newspaper at one point, and it's heartbreaking what's being done to it right now, what kind of crude nonsense it's being used to publish. It may be a more unfortunate fate than the way *City Paper* was snuffed out of existence entirely.

This book is in no small part built on the foundation of work that I and other excellent journalists did for *City Paper* and the *Baltimore Sun*. Since that work is now paywalled on the *Sun*'s website, if it's still online at all, it exists to profit David D. Smith's empire of Republican propaganda. So I'm extremely happy to synthesize that journalism and make it available to you elsewhere. Since 2022, I've also continued to cover Baltimore music for the *Sun*'s newer competitor, the *Baltimore Banner*, thanks to editors including Lawrence Burney and Caitlin Moore, and I hope I can continue to write about this city's arts and culture for as long as I live, even though my wife and I moved outside the city to Laurel, Maryland, for her work.

Cutting my teeth in the alt-weekly world, writing for not just *Baltimore City Paper* but also the *Village Voice* and *City Pages* and the *Washington City Paper* and other venerable weekly papers, was incredibly valuable training. I'm proud to have become a writer in that world, and I think it's a tremendous loss that far fewer current and future writers will have the opportunity to learn their craft in that space.

"Local" is sometimes seen as a shameful or insulting word in music media, but treating the music that's made in your neck of the woods with curiosity and respect is incredibly rewarding, and too many music writers have never even tried it. Fun music and dance music deserve thoughtful journalism and critical analysis as much as more conventionally "serious" art. A lot of silly or ostensibly meaningless records hold a lot of meaning to me. The label, the producer, the year it was made, who was copying whose styles, who was expanding on that. And as a White writer documenting a predominantly Black genre, I don't take it for granted that a lot of people have allowed me to tell their stories, and that there is always a huge amount of racial and cultural subtext to navigate and acknowledge. I took that responsibility seriously and am grateful to everyone I spoke to for this book and the articles that I drew on for the book.

Let me thank all the Kickstarter backers: Dan Gibson, Chris Merriam, Job de Wit, alsteed, Evan Cunningham, bartligthart, Jeff Reguilon, Dwayne Lawson, Christopher R. Weingarten, Mat Leffler-Schulman, Mike Bartolomeo, Kelly Connelly, Brandon Lackey, Ian Ward Comfort, Brandon Soderberg, John Heikel, PenDragon, Austin Stahl, JoAnn Bacher, Mike Bacher, Martha Heikel, Michaelangelo Matos, Marc Gilman, Albert, Emaline Shipley, Chris Burlingame, Nick Minichino, Jillian Teller, Logan K. Young, Dean Jackson, Edward, Steve Newsense, Josh Brown, Cynthia Heikel, tomred, Harvey Rhames, Richard Shipley, Michael Byrne, Robert Korwek, Say Wut, Crystal Tennessee, Jade Fox, and MsTris Beats.

There are a lot of friends and family members in the above

list, and there are a lot more wonderful people in my life and in the Baltimore scene and in the music writer community that I haven't mentioned, including about 50 people that I interviewed and quoted in this book. I'm not really a social butterfly – I don't go out a lot, I'm always a little wrapped up in my work, and people who I consider dear friends sometimes go far too long without hearing from me. But as I write this, I'm a little amazed at how many people have had a positive impact on me and my life over the last 15 or 20 years during which I slowly made my way towards this moment, many more than just the ones I've named here.

Accept my apologies if I didn't shout you out by name – it'd be impossible to mention everybody, and I'd rather allow the list to be incomplete than to try and fail to be comprehensive. But I will close by thanking my family. My mother, Cynthia Heikel, always allowed and encouraged me to follow my love of music, and helped me get my first drum set and fill her house with noise. My brother, Zac Shipley, was right there with me starting bands and buying CDs at the Sound Garden and reading *City Paper*. One year, my mother-in-law Sue German and brother-in-law John German gave me a Sony IC recorder for my birthday, and I've recorded hundreds of interviews with it, including most of the interviews conducted for this book.

My wife, Jennifer German, and our sons, James and Daniel, have made me smile every day, and one or all of them has been in the room with me practically every time I've worked on the book. We live in an imperfect and often frustrating world, but I've lived an extremely happy life because of the people around me, and I appreciate you all.

Chapter 1
You'll Know If You Belong

"It was just dance music, it was no specific genre," says Wayne Davis, one of the first working club DJs in Baltimore. "It could come from any genre, as long as it was danceable music." French discotheque culture had become popular in American cities in the 1960s, but the idea of "disco" as a genre of music unto itself did not become a widely embraced music industry category until the mid-'70s.

First, there were just disc jockeys, figuring out what music people enjoyed dancing to, one song at a time. The job of a disc jockey primarily existed in radio broadcasting — previously, live bands and jukeboxes had provided most of the music in bars and clubs. But that was beginning to change as more and more DJs began to provide a tailored selection of songs for the clientele of various venues, bars, and restaurants.

David Mancuso's Manhattan club the Loft is remembered as the unofficial birthplace of disco, where Mancuso pioneered the idea of a continuous stream of music, with songs with similar tempos mixed together on two turntables, in the early '70s. DJ Kool Herc had the parallel innovation of bringing Jamaican sound system culture to the Bronx, spinning records at parties beginning in 1973 that would eventually blossom into hip hop. Baltimore is just a four-hour drive from New York, and Wayne Davis was inspired to become a DJ after making the trip up I-95 and going to the Loft.

"I was exposed to i, by going to a couple of events in New York with a friend that took me up there that was into the scene," says Davis. "She took me to the Loft, and maybe a couple other [clubs] I don't remember the names of, but that's where I saw the people blending music, using two [records]."

Davis, born in 1952, has been the most continuously active and influential figure in dance music in Baltimore for over half a century, working at and/or owning several of the venues where Baltimore club music slowly developed out of house music into a genre unto itself. As the fatherly and eventually grandfatherly presence that has presided over the scene, though, Davis is nearly 20 years older than many of the producers who created the first wave of club music, and his sensibility is rooted in house and earlier styles. "It was just me building a place with the things that I thought were important," Davis says of his clubs. "And out of that, I created a canvas for a lot of their creativity."

When Davis began DJing, major labels were still years away from embracing dance clubs and catering to DJs with 12" singles for optimal mixing. So he would mix with whatever he had in his record collection, often smaller 7" singles or individual songs from a 12" album, including more cutting-edge dance music from European labels that American record stores would import. "When I started, I was using 45s, the little ones that had the hole in the middle, or two albums, playing a track off an album," he says. Davis and two friends would host "theme parties" around the city, for which he would curate the music, and that was where he met Odell Brock Jr.

Odell Brock Jr., born in 1945, had worked for Brock Fuel Oil and Oil Burner Service, a company owned by his father, Odell Brock Sr. In 1972, Brock Jr. opened the Carousel with business partner David H. Richeson. The venue, located at 1815 North Charles Street, initially focused on hosting concerts with live bands. "Then Odell came up with the concept of doing a discotheque, that's when I was brought in," Davis remembers.

The technology that today's DJs take for granted was still being developed and invented, one club at a time, in the early '70s. A modern DJ would have a mixing board, with fader dials to gradually fade from the record on one turntable to the other, and headphones to listen a song before it was faded in on the dancefloor speakers. Davis did not have those luxuries. "At the Carousel, they didn't even have a mixer in there at first. They had a toggle switch and two turntables. I introduced them to a person that had some sound knowledge, because they had a Radio Shack system in there," Davis says. "They didn't have any clue that a DJ needed to hear, and they had a little booth that was sealed all the way up to the top with plexiglass. I had to stick my head out the door to hear when to click the toggle switch over for the next record."

The Hippo, a gay bar located on Charles Street, about nine blocks south of the Carousel, also opened in 1972. "I was the first DJ to play at the Hippo," Davis says. "A guy at the Hippo, Steve Johnson, built a mixer, that was the first mixer that I used."

Davis's weekly Wednesday night gig at the Hippo didn't last long, however, and it would be years before the bar hired other DJs. "My crowd was kind of a diverse crowd, and they weren't too comfortable with that. So they eliminated me, and then Steve Johnson paired two jukeboxes so that people would make their selection, and it would be continuous, but just not mixed."

New York's disco culture reveled in the idea of a multicultural utopia of different people dancing together,

White and Black, straight and queer. Baltimore was an East Coast city with similar demographics, but it was distinctly more working class, and its racial tensions were a little more fraught. Baltimore rioted, like many other American cities, after the assassination of Martin Luther King Jr. in April 1968. Baltimore's riots lasted nine days, resulting in six deaths and thousands of arrests. The "White flight" of middle-class White Baltimoreans to the surrounding suburbs in Baltimore County accelerated in the '70s, and at some point in the decade, Baltimore became a majority-Black city for the first time. African Americans accounted for 54.8% of the city's residents in the 1980 U.S. census, and that number reached a high of 64% in the 2000 census.

The Hippo played its own significant role in Baltimore's counterculture and dance music, but it evidently wasn't yet ready for the music, or the clientele, that Davis was bringing to the Carousel and a succession of clubs that followed. The Hippo closed in 2015, and the building where it stood is now a CVS drug store.

In 1976, Odell Brock sold his interest in the Carousel to Richeson, who renamed it Gatsby's. Then Brock opened his eponymous club, a bigger room just around the corner, with Davis as the club's first DJ. The 18,000-square-foot building at 21 E. North Avenue was built in 1909, and had been nightclub on and off since 1940, but it wasn't a legendary staple of Baltimore nightlife until it became Odell's Nightclub. The entrance to Odell's greeted visitors with the motto "You'll know if you belong." And over the next decade, many felt like they belonged, as Brock and Davis taught a generation of Black Baltimoreans how to love dance music in all its forms.

Each of the four nights of the week that Odell's was open had a slightly different musical slant and a different target audience.

"The college party was Thursday night. Friday kinda started bein' established as when we'd play more of the import stuff. And then Saturday night was more just a blend of everything," Davis says. The Hippo may have been anxious about drawing too much of a Black crowd, but Odell's had no hesitation about welcoming a queer crowd on a weekly basis. "Monday night was gay night there, it was just called 'gay night.'"

Odell Brock's first name became iconic in Baltimore because of his club, and even today "Odell's" is used as shorthand to evoke an era and a musical aesthetic. There are countless mixtapes and DJ mixes with "Odell's" in the title to signify early Baltimore club music and its precursors, often made by DJs who never worked in the club.

Brock wasn't a DJ himself, though, and didn't have much influence on what the DJs at Odell's played. Odell's had a capacity of about one thousand. There was another dancefloor on the second floor where Brock's friends and younger brother sometimes DJed, but Davis was, for many years, the maestro of the main room. "[Odell] didn't have input on what I played. He would sometimes come to the booth and try to tell me things, but I didn't pay him any attention," Davis says. And Brock's friends didn't actually call him Odell. "'Pee Wee' was his nickname. When I met him, that's what they would call him, 'Pee Wee.'" Try to imagine, for a moment, a parallel universe where Baltimore's most legendary club was called Pee Wee's.

Odell's original sound system was initially provided by Flite Three Studios, a Baltimore company that was also one of the first local labels to release disco records, by founder W. Craig Kenney and the group Belle Farms Estates.

Eventually, though, Odell's sought out the services of Richard Long, the sound designer who'd created bass-heavy sound systems for famed New York discos like the Paradise Garage and Studio 54. Long had worked with pioneering DJ Larry Levan to develop the ground-shaking subwoofer known as "Larry's horn" at the Paradise Garage. As disco became a mainstream monolith in the late '70s, Odell's spent a decade cultivating the kind of eclectic mix of dance music that remained on the outer reaches of the Billboard charts, or outside them entirely, that had been minted in the Loft and other legendary underground clubs like the Warehouse in Chicago, the namesake of the house music genre.

Disco, recorded primarily by bands and session musicians with conventional instruments, reached a saturation point and began to suffer a backlash and commercial decline in the early '80s. House music, featuring the theoretically more flawless and steady grooves of drum machines, sequencers, and loops, became the quirkier, dirtier, and frequently lower-fidelity successor to disco in underground clubs, particularly in Chicago and New York.

Record pools, organizations that would distribute new vinyl to club and radio DJs for a membership fee, started to become part of dance music's growing national ecosystem. But there were no record pools in Baltimore at the time, so Davis joined a record pool in Washington, D.C., an hour's drive away. "I used to go there to pick up my records once a week," he says. "It was more just finding danceable music to my ear that I liked."

"I have a diverse ear," Davis says. "As a DJ, I won the trust of people. So as long as I gave them something familiar when I played something new, it didn't clear the floor, because they trusted that it was gonna be something they enjoyed."

While New York discos could keep the party going all night in "the city that never sleeps," Baltimore laws regarding the operating hours of bars and clubs were more restrictive, and Odell Brock found a creative solution to that problem. "In Baltimore, you had to close at 2 o'clock," his wife Jacqueline Brock told *Baltimore Fishbowl* in 2021. "He said, 'Well, we'll just serve punch.' So that's how we were able to stay open until 4, 5 o'clock in the morning. And people were still not ready to go home." The Odell's model, an after-hours club with no liquor license serving punch, would endure for decades in Baltimore. Brock opened other nightspots, including the Ritz on Light Street and D'Joint on Liberty Road, but Odell's remained his claim to fame.

"I was a young kid at this club called Odell's, and it was playing this kind of music that you never heard anywhere else," said Thommy Davis (no relation to Wayne Davis) in an interview with the podcast *The Truth In This Art* in 2024. In the early '80s, the music at Odell's could vary from lesser-known hits from the dance and R&B charts (groups like First Choice and Inner Life) to British synth pop and new wave (the Thompson Twins and Peter Godwin). One of those underground dance staples was "Is It All Over My Face" by Loose Joints, an Arthur Russell production featuring vocals by dancers from the Loft, which became a foundational work of house music. All of this was colloquially referred to as "club music" in Baltimore long before "Baltimore club music" became a genre unto itself of locally produced records.

"There was all kinds of music being played in the club. There was Sugar Hill Gang, there was house music, there was all kinds of music. So when I started DJing there was a mesh of music. I played everything from Kraftwerk to Trouble Funk, everything in between, Depeche Mode," says Teddy Douglas. Douglas, born in 1964, would form the legendary house music production team the Basement Boys with Thommy Davis and

Jay Steinhour. "At the clubs I hung at like the Paradise Garage, if it was danceable, it was played."

"My first club was Odell's, and for the first year I worked there I didn't get paid a dollar. You gotta pay your dues in this business," says DJ Mike Crosby. Even in the club's later years, when hip hop was becoming commercially dominant, Crosby remembers that dance music still ruled supreme at Odell's. "All you would play is club all night, and then at 2 o'clock, 15 minutes of hip hop."

While the crack epidemic had changed urban life in many American cities in the early '80s and led to higher crime rates, heroin was the drug that had Baltimore in a chokehold, and crack didn't make a major impact in Maryland until the end of the decade. The happy memories that Baltimoreans of a certain age have of Odell's focus on the music and the dancing, and during Brock's tenure running the club, Odell's endured little controversy. Unfortunately, the socioeconomic issues that plagued Baltimore in the '80s became part of the club's downfall.

Brock had taken on loans and new business partners to fund multiple renovations to improve the space and the sound system at Odell's. "He tried to take it upscale and kinda market it to his peers, and that's when he made a loan," says Davis. Brock, who had terminal cancer, sold his club to Phillip "Phil Boy" Murray in July 1984. Odell Brock Jr. died on December 13th, 1984, at the age of 39, survived by his wife and their three daughters.

Odell's continued operating under the same name but under much more turbulent circumstances. 50 federal agents descended on Odell's at 7pm on December 3rd, 1987, confiscating business records and a shotgun. Murray was indicted, and eventually convicted, in a criminal conspiracy alongside one of his business partners, William "Little Will" Franklin, who had been identified a decade earlier as one of the biggest heroin dealers in Baltimore. Odell's had become a money-laundering front for a drug empire.

Davis arrived at Odell's to work that night and found that the feds had closed the club and put padlocks on the doors. "I had a party planned that night, I was bringing in a DJ from the New Jersey/New York area," he remembers. "I knew the guys that had [the club] were from the street, but I didn't know that all that was going on."

The next owner of Odell's, Milton Tillman Jr., was also bad news. "They reopened maybe about a year later," Davis says. "It was a whole different genre, different people, different root, and they started becoming a nuisance in the neighborhood." Over the lifespan of Odell's, at least half a dozen people were shot and killed in front of the club. In the summer of 1992, five people were wounded outside Odell's in a shooting incident, and the *Baltimore Sun* ran an editorial urging the city government to "throw the book at Odell's." Instead, it was federal law enforcement that once again shut the club down a few weeks later.

Odell's was raided by the FBI on September 1st, 1992, this time as part of a corruption investigation. Odell's closed for the last time in 1993 when Tillman was sentenced to 27 months in prison for attempting to bribe a Baltimore zoning board member. The club's Richard Long sound system wound up in another club owned by Tillman, Trilogy on Eutaw Street. Tillman was sentenced to prison again in 2011, after being convicted of operating as a bail bondsman without a license.

The Odell's building stood vacant on North Avenue for 25 years, until developers purchased it in 2017. Over $6 million was invested in renovating the building, and it was reopened in 2021 as the home of two non-profit organizations: Arts for Learning Maryland and Code in the Schools. Odell Brock Jr.'s family was invited to the dance party commemorating the reopening, and one wall in the offices is adorned with photos and memorabilia from the building's past life as a dance music mecca. Given all the crime and controversy that Odell's was associated with after its founder and namesake's death, it's heartening that the club is remembered for its music and community.

Odell's was already in its troubled later years when local producers began releasing the records that would come to be known as Baltimore club music. But countless future club music producers, including Rod Lee and Kevin "K-Life" Shanks, had their eyes opened to dance music by Odell's DJs like Wayne Davis, Teddy Douglas, and Sean Marshall. "Sean Marshall is the one that got me likin' club music. Me and K-Life went to Odell's," Rod Lee says. "I never went out to the clubs, all my homeboys were like, 'Yo, you need to go to clubs.' I was like, 'Nah, I don't wanna go.' And this one particular time, I walked in there, it was a wrap."

Chapter 2
Git the Hole

Just as many of the kids who picked up a guitar in the 1960s have similar stories of being entranced by the Beatles on *The Ed Sullivan Show*, the DJs who came of age in the 1980s, including the ones who would help develop Baltimore club music, often have formative memories of the same seminal moments for hip hop and DJ culture.

In February 1981, the Bronx group Funky Four + 1 became the first hip hop group to perform on "Saturday Night Live," at the invitation of the episode's host, Blondie's Debbie Harry. In contrast to what would become conventional hip hop concert staging, with the MCs in the front and the DJ in back, "SNL" positioned DJ Breakout right out front, while the group's five rappers performed behind him. It was doubtless the first time many people saw a DJ operate two turntables and a mixer like a musical instrument, and Eric "DJ Kool Breez" Atwell was one of those kids, at home in Essex, Maryland. "I started DJin' when I was, like, fuckin' 11," says Kool Breez, who was born in 1972. "By the time I was 13, I was getting paid to do parties."

Glenn "DJ Technics" Brand was inspired by the earliest local hip hop crews that would put on block parties and DJ on the radio. "Comin' up in Baltimore, I was influenced heavily by DJ Spen, the Numarx, Jeffrey C, Terry T, We Rock Krew, AP Crew, just anybody that was out on WWIN and WEBB back in the day, I pretty much came up under that lineage of DJs in Baltimore," Technics said in a 2023 YouTube interview produced by BV 1103 Films. "I came up in the '80s watching DJs out in Druid Hill Park play music with six or eight turntables, makin' people move, and I thought to myself, 'I think that's something I can do.'"

"1982 is when I finally decided to venture into DJing, but I'd been collecting records since 1977, so I already had musical knowledge and a collection, I just needed the tools to start trying things together," said Technics. "By about 10 or 11 years old, I already had records the way people have Jordans now, they were just stacked up high, and I needed to figure out exactly how I was gonna utilize the music outside of just collecting it."

Scott "Scottie B." Rice was born in 1968 into the heavily Jewish community that had settled within Park Heights in northwest Baltimore in the first half of the twentieth century. His great-great grandfather had been the first ordained rabbi in the United States, but Scottie's passion from an early age was music. Scottie B. made his unofficial debut as a DJ at ten years old, "playing the records for the school plays" (he only had one turntable, property of Baltimore City Public Schools).

He didn't start to seriously consider DJing as a vocation, however, until Funky Four + 1's label, Sugar Hill Records, released the groundbreaking 1981 single "The Adventures of Grandmaster Flash on the Wheels of Steel." The seven-minute tour de force featured the first true rock star of hip hop DJing, Grandmaster Flash, mixing several records on three turntables while showcasing all of his tricks of the trade, some of which he pioneered: scratching, cutting, rubbing, and crossfading. "Oh yeah, that's some shit I wanna do," Scottie B. remembers thinking.

A friend's older brother came back from living in New York City and regaled Scottie with descriptions of competitive mixing contests he witnessed, and tried to demonstrate some of those fancy techniques. "He sounded terrible, but it was like, 'Oh, this is like what the Grandmaster Flash record was.'"

When Scottie B. began to DJ at house parties and rec centers as a teenager, dance music was in a transitional period. "It was like the precursor to house, whatever you call the music in between disco and house, you know, electro-ish kinda stuff, breaks. Arthur Baker, that was big," he says. Baker was the producer who sampled Kraftwerk on Afrika Bambataa's "Planet Rock" and became one of the first pro remixers who'd make official dance mixes for major-label hits by the likes of Cyndi Lauper and Bruce Springsteen.

As a lifelong devotee of hip hop and house music, Scottie B. still tends to wear a ballcap, an XL T-shirt, and shorts when I see him around the city. Comfortable anywhere in Baltimore as an active DJ in the city for over 40 years straight, Scottie B. is nonchalant and even self-deprecating about the scene he helped develop with his mostly Black friends and peers in the '80s and '90s.

Scottie B. started building his vinyl collection at Metro Stereo in nearby Reisterstown Plaza (which later changed locations to Mondawmin Mall). Thommy Davis worked at Metro Stereo and became one of the first people that Scottie met in Baltimore's growing DJ scene. A friend who lived in the area, Daniel Woodis Jr., would eventually become DJ Class and record for a label founded by Scottie. Birdland was another store Scottie would occasionally catch a ride to, "because my father used to always go down to get us food stamps and stuff."

Over in Northeast Baltimore, a few miles away, another group of kids who'd eventually record for Scottie B.'s label began forging a lifelong bond over music. Grant "DJ Booman" Burley, born in 1972, was the son of a member of the Baltimore vocal quintet the Mighty Mondells. Burley's family lived on the Alameda, two doors down from Jimmy Jones, born in 1970. Jones's grandmother lived in Morgan Park near Kenneth "K.W. Griff" Wilkins, born in 1971.

"I think I may have met [Booman] during my junior high years," says the well-dressed and bespectacled Griff, a suave and easygoing guy who for decades has been an accountant by day and a DJ by night.

"[Griff] was DJin' before I was. He actually DJed my first house party," says Booman, heavyset and dark-skinned with a cleanly shaven head, more casual in sweats at the end of a long day. "I was tryin' to figure out what to do, but he came through and really did the party, because I only had one turntable," he says with a laugh. It was a Realistic turntable, a brand produced by Radio Shack. "They definitely weren't 1200s. Straight arm, no pitch control."

Changa Bell was "kind of the glue between a lot of us, early on," according to Booman. Bell, who rapped at the time, and later found success as a professional life coach and the founder of the Black Male Yoga Initiative, introduced both Booman and Griff to one of his Calvert Hall classmates, Shawn Caesar, who'd eventually co-found the label that would release their earliest music. "I remember the first time I met Shawn Ceasar, it wasn't through music, he was playing football," Booman says. "I remember him having a mohawk and just being crazy and running around, like he was just a football guy. And I think I later found out he DJed."

Booman, Griff, and Jones started hanging out in record stores in Northeast Baltimore, before gravitating towards the downtown spots where the city's DJ scene was coalescing. "There was a store called Cozy Corner Records in Northwood, that was kinda like the focal point for everybody," Griff remembers. "That's where we got most of our records from, before we got a little older and started learning about these other stores and being introduced to other DJs. We wound up being all over the place, downtown, Music Liberated, a lot of record stores, man."

Bernie Rabinowitz, born in 1942, opened the first Music Liberated with his brother Jerry Rabinowitz on Charles Street in the late '60s, eventually expanding it to a chain of six stores, including locations in Mondawmin Mall, in Federal Hill, and in Towson in Baltimore County.

When house music took hold in Baltimore in the '80s, Music Liberated was one of the first stores that catered heavily to the 12" singles that every DJ needed to fill their crates with to start a party. Rabinowitz often employed people like DJ Technics who were both knowledgeable about the merchandise and able to DJ in the store during shopping hours to entertain customers and get them interested in buying particular records.

"All the house, all the imported stuff from the UK, and all those records we ended up sampling, all that stuff was coming from there," Booman says.

"They cost about 20 dollars! All we needed was about five seconds off of it, so we had to buy two of 'em," Griff adds with a laugh.

"Yup, they were expensive. Regular singles were maybe like

five bucks or something like that, but those imports, you easily paid 20 bucks, it was crazy," Booman says.

"If Bernie didn't have a DJ in the store at the time you were there, he would let you go and play records while the customers were in there and stuff, so that was cool," Griff remembers.

Robert "DJ Equalizer" Marianos, born in 1967, started working at Music Liberated as a teenager in the mid-'80s, and was, alongside Technics, instrumental in Rabinowitz's move towards stocking dance singles. "Bernie and his brother had already had that store for umpteen years prior to me even hooking up with him," Equalizer remembers. "But when I hooked up with him, I ended up becoming the buyer for all the stores they had. And they were the biggest game in town. They weren't the only game, but they were the biggest and most powerful. Next thing you know I'm managing the stores, I'm doing the buying for all the music, not just 12-inches."

DJ Equalizer isn't one of the most widely recognized names in Baltimore club music, but he's one of the most important figures in the genre's early development, someone that all of his contemporaries credit as a trailblazer. He's also one of the scene's more bombastic personalities, someone who isn't afraid to make sweeping proclamations, like "I created the DJ business, literally, in this city. I mean, totally turned it into a business."

Equalizer's old friend and sometime competitor, Scottie B., speaks in the matter-of-fact, deadpan tone of a guy who's seen it all. He's humbler about his own significant role in Baltimore club music. "We were trying to make music that would fit into the parties that we were playing," Scottie B. told the *True Laurels* zine in 2014. "We had an idea of what worked but we weren't thinking outside the box. It was really small-minded.

We thought on weekly terms, like what we could play at our next gig."

Eventually, Equalizer started his own store, Inner City Records, which also became an important hub for the local DJ scene. "I left Bernie after a couple years, I moved away from him, and I started a chain of stores. And I ended up shutting down two of Bernie's stores, and I feel bad about that, because that wasn't the point," Equalizer says. Scottie B., DJ Class, and Rod Lee were among the notable DJs that worked at Inner City stores.

"I remember thinking, y'know, why are people afraid to do this for a living? You should be able to do this as a regular job, you should be able to make a living as a DJ," Equalizer says.

> "Now way back when it was all startin' off, there was only three or four regular DJs in the city that actually had a name and would play the biggest clubs and on the radio. And that was a good buddy of mine, Pumpin Paul, Frank Ski, myself, and Thommy Davis. And we were professionals at it."

In 1987, Thommy Davis released what has been called the first Baltimore club record, or is at the very least the first underground house record from a Baltimore artist, "Git the Hole," on his independent label Thomix Records. "Git the Hole," sometimes released as "Git Da Hole," was primarily built on a sample of "Can You Move," a 1981 Odell's staple from the British new wave group Modern Romance, and also featured a loop of the very recognizable "Yeah!" that opened the Beastie Boys' 1986 hit "(You Gotta) Fight For Your Right (To Party)." The artist name that "Git the Hole" was credited to in the US was Dem N****s – in the UK, the credited artist was simply Thomas Davis.

With its raw mix of percussion, bass, and stuttering vocal loops, "Git the Hole" is an impressively prescient forerunner of the sound that would dominate Baltimore dancefloors in the years to follow. It differs from its descendants in a couple of key respects, however: at 116 beats per minute, it's noticeably slower than Baltimore club's eventual standard tempo, 130 BPM, and relies primarily on a drum machine instead of a breakbeat.

In 1988, Thommy Davis's group, the Basement Boys, scored a national hit with "Love Don't Live Here No More," on Jump Street Records, reaching #25 on *Billboard*'s Dance Club Play chart. In 1989, Davis left the Basement Boys and was replaced by Sean "DJ Spen" Spencer, who'd been a member of one of Baltimore's first notable hip hop groups, Numarx.

Numarx made straight up rap songs, but also dabbled in house music and R&B ballads, including a song called "Girl You Know It's True," their attempt at something in the vein of LL Cool J's groundbreaking hip hop love song "I Need Love." In 1989, "Girl You Know It's True" was covered by the ascendant pop duo Milli Vanilli, and became a worldwide hit. One of the other members of Numarx who co-wrote the song, Kevin Liles, would go on to become a high-ranking executive at labels like Def Jam, Warner Music Group, and 300 Entertainment. One of the last Numarx tracks released before the group disbanded, 1991's "Drop Downt to Your Knees (North Avenue Mix)" became a beloved club staple in Baltimore.

In the '90s, the Basement Boys would produce a series of house anthems for singers like New Jersey's Crystal Waters ("Gypsy Woman," "100% Pure Love") and Baltimore's Ultra Nate ("Free," "Show Me") that thrived on *Billboard*'s dance charts. The Basement Boys/Numarx axis of Baltimore house and hip hop was moving towards dance music's mainstream, while another set of Baltimore DJs and musicians were tunneling further underground, creating something that, for many years, had Baltimore dancefloors in a frenzy without finding much recognition outside Maryland.

During the Great Migration between 1910 and 1970, millions of Black Americans moved from the Deep South to other regions of the country, particularly Northeastern cities, including Baltimore. Baltimore played an integral but often underestimated role in Black American music throughout the twentieth century. For decades, major jazz and R&B stars would frequently perform at venues in the Pennsylvania Avenue entertainment district, or the Famous Ballroom on Charles Street. Legends like Billie Holiday and Cab Calloway grew up in Baltimore, though they had to leave the city to become famous. That has often been true of subsequent generations of Baltimore musicians who've had to move away, tour heavily, or seek out music industry connections elsewhere to achieve commercial success.

The Buddy Deane Show, a teen dance show on local Baltimore television in the '50s and '60s, helped turn the Twist into one of the biggest dance crazes in American history. But civil rights era tensions loomed large over the show: most episodes featured only White teenagers, with all Black dancers every other Friday. John Waters loosely based his hit film *Hairspray* on *The Buddy Deane Show*, although in real life the show went off the air without ever desegregating its dancers.

From 1820 to 1850, Baltimore was the second-most populous city in America after New York City. By 1950, Baltimore reached its peak population of nearly a million residents, while New York had rocketed to a population of over seven million. Baltimore's population has declined in 74 of the last 75 years – the exception, 2014, has been attributed in part to a dip in the city's murder rate. Today, there are a little over half a million residents, making it the 30th-most populous city in America, right between Memphis and Milwaukee.

In the '80s, the few Baltimore acts that signed contracts with big labels or scored mainstream hits were primarily White rock bands like Kix and the Ravyns – although Stargate, a funk band from Anne Arundel County, not far outside the city, also enjoyed commercial success. The lack of music industry attention around Baltimore meant that anyone there with a new sound had to build up their own labels, their own studios, their own venues, their own record stores, their own fanbases, their own radio shows. And that's what the Baltimore club community did. Although several key figures in early Baltimore club music were White – including DJ Equalizer, Scottie B., DJ Kool Breez, DJ Big Red, and DJ Excel – the overwhelming majority of the people making and consuming the music were Black, and over the course of the '90s it would become a grassroots phenomenon of working-class Black Baltimore, a symbol of the city's irreverent and indefatigable spirit.

Chapter 3
Think (About It)

From the development of the earliest tape loops and rudimentary drum machines over 60 years ago, popular music has undergone a slow, gradual transition. Before that transition, most songs on the pop charts were built upon rhythm tracks played by human drummers. After that transition, many if not most songs have been built upon looped or programmed beats, or at the very least with drummers playing along with steady click tracks, allowing their performances to be edited to metronomic perfection. The biggest leaps that technology took to allow that transition came about during the 1980s, and the changes took root first in hip hop and dance music.

DJs and beatmakers had freed music from the necessity of the band, and from the drum set specifically – not maliciously, despite how some drummers may have felt at the time. In fact, many DJs created their best rhythm tracks by looping a human drummer's work. The breakbeat is, simply put, the "break" in a record where most of the instruments and singers on the song go silent for a bar or two while the drummer keeps the rhythm going (and maybe gets in some tasty licks). A breakbeat doesn't have to consist solely of drums, but the drummer is the reason most DJs or producers isolate a breakbeat – to have a rhythm track to dance to, or to make an entirely new song out of.

Early hip hop DJs would keep the break going as long

as possible, usually by toggling between two copies of the same record, a feat of showmanship akin to keeping several spinning plates in the air at once. The dancers who got busy with their flashiest moves during those moments took their name from breakbeats, and break dancing became one of the core elements of hip hop culture.

As samplers became more affordable in the '80s and many DJs moved into producing original records of their own, looping a breakbeat infinitely, without having to cut between two copies of a record, became an artform unto itself. Many breakbeats came from obscure records, or the least recognizable parts of popular records, and the musicians whose records had been sampled were often uncredited and uncompensated, at least in the '80s, when there were few laws or standard industry practices regarding samples.

DJs dug deep in the vinyl crates in record stores to find the best breaks and discover new breaks, not to merely pull crowd-pleasing breaks from hit records that people already knew. If there was any reliable brand name in breakbeats, however, it was James Brown. The Godfather of Soul had provided the soundtrack for a generation of Black Americans with his remarkable run of hits from 1956 through the mid-'70s – he made intermittent comebacks afterwards, but the smooth four-on-the-floor beat of disco helped push the busy, syncopated funk grooves of Brown's bands off the charts. Once the hip hop producers of the '80s had samplers and sampling keyboards at their disposal, though, their parents' James Brown records became the raw material with which to create something new.

James Brown samples abound in every era of rap, but the period from 1987 to 1989 was the peak of Brown's grip on the hip hop nation. In that three-year span, 1970's "Funky

Drummer" alone was sampled on a staggering array of classic songs by Public Enemy, Run-DMC, N.W.A, Boogie Down Productions, Eric B. & Rakim, De La Soul, Beastie Boys, DJ Jazzy Jeff & the Fresh Prince, and Stetsasonic – to say nothing of all the other rap songs of that era that sampled other Brown tracks like "Hot Pants" or "Get Up, Get Into It, Get Involved."

James Brown was infamous for how tightly he ran his backing band, (usually known as the J.B.'s), drilling musicians who often had no formal training with lengthy rehearsals, and even fining them when they made errors during performances. In the very best years of James Brown's output, from 1965 to 1970, the J.B.'s featured two drummers, allowing the rhythm section to construct complex polyrhythms and follow Brown's gestures and dance moves while still holding down a steady beat. Clyde Stubblefield was the titular drummer on "Funky Drummer," and he quit Brown's band along with several other musicians in 1970 over a pay dispute. The other drummer, the Alabama-born John "Jabo" Starks, remained with Brown through 1975, at which point he went to work for blues legend B.B. King, a less strict bandleader whose music required more relaxed grooves.

In the early '70s, James Brown started his own label, People Records, which primarily released records by his many collaborators and protégés, including instrumental albums by the J.B.'s. The most successful solo artist on People Records was Gloria Lavern Collins, a Texas girl who became the lead female vocalist in Brown's stage show after sending him a demo tape. As Lyn Collins, she began releasing Brown-produced solo singles in 1971, and in 1972, "Think (About It)" became the first of her three Hot 100 hits, peaking at #66.

Written and produced by Brown with the J.B.'s backing

Collins, "Think (About It)" is a DJ's dream. Despite Collins's starmaking vocal performance, the three-minute track features several pockets of empty space where Jabo Starks's drums take center stage. In fact, there are five distinct breakbeats in "Think" that have been sampled on many occasions, most of them featuring vocal ad libs performed by unidentified J.B.'s (Brown's voice is intermittently recognizable on the song, though he isn't responsible for the song's most famous ad libs). At the 1-minute-and-22-second mark, one musician shouts a gruff "Yeah!" that one of his bandmates answers with a high-pitched "Woo!" At 2 minutes and 17 seconds, one J.B. hollers some words of encouragement to Collins: "Ya bad, sister!"

Every drummer has certain signature rhythms in their bones that they return to over and over, and the shuffle that drives "Think (About It)" is all Jabo Starks. Variations on that particular rhythm abound in Brown's catalog – you can even hear Starks play a slower but basically identical version of the same groove on the 1974 track "Mind Power."

The most sampled sections of "Think (About It)" are relatively simple and straightforward – a 4/4 bar with the snare on the 2 and the 4 – but the asymmetry of where Starks places the rhythmic accents gives it a hypnotic forward motion, especially when looped. The bass drum thumps hard on the 1, but the second snare hit lands much louder than the first with a flam (both sticks striking the drumhead slightly out of sync, the second stick harder than the first). In between those two snare hits, Starks plays a few shuffling ghost notes that sync up with the 16th notes being played by a persistently rattling tambourine.

All of this means that the "Think" breakbeat is in constant motion, but it always seems to be building to that big snare flam at the end of the bar, immediately followed by the fat kick drum that opens the next bar. If you're dancing to any of the thousands of Baltimore tracks with "Think" as its central engine, you can lean into the same beats that Starks leans into, always with confidence that you'll land firmly back on the one just like his kick drum. It swings more than any drum machine track could, and, for that matter, it swings more than most of the breakbeats that made it into the house music canon.

Sampling is often thought of as a lazy way of making music, or an opportunistic way of scoring a hit with a secondhand sound or hook that already worked once before. But a record with a sample, good or bad, is a time capsule that contains multiple moments from different places and eras. A Baltimore club record with a "Think" break contains the thousands of hours Starks spent finding that pocket and perfecting it, in addition to whatever ideas the producer of the new song added on top of it. Two people who've never met are collaborating, even if one of them is likely completely unaware of it. Brown got the take he needed, and Starks walked out of the session like any other day on the job, but the groove they captured continues to birth new songs on a daily basis.

The Rosetta Stone that helped spread "Think (About It)," "Funky Drummer," the "Amen" break (from the Winstons' "Amen Brother"), and countless other drum loops to DJs in Baltimore and around the world was *Ultimate Breaks and Beats*, a series of 12"s released by the New York label Street Beat Records from 1986 to 1991. Many hip hop and dance records took samples straight from the source, but innumerable classics sampled directly from the 25 volumes of *Ultimate Breaks and Beats*. Most of the breaks featured in the series were already popular and in demand among DJs and producers, but the popularity of the Street Beat compilations amplified many of those tracks and made them into staples, including the edit of "Think (About It)" by Louis "Breakbeat Lou" Flores that appeared on the 16th volume.

In the early '90s, DJ Equalizer expanded the Inner City Records brand from a retail store to a label (Inner City Records Co., to distinguish it from the Inner City Records that began releasing jazz albums in 1976). Inspired by Street Beat, Equalizer created his own series of breakbeat collections under the cheeky title *Beats, Breaks & Bullshit*, which probably equaled the impact of *Ultimate Breaks* among Baltimore DJs. "He had some really, really influential breaks," says Diamond K. The second *Bullshit* EP contained "Bad Sister," which was for a time the most dominant "Think (About It)" edit in Baltimore club tracks – to this day, many Baltimore producers refer to the sample as "Ya Bad Sister" rather than "Think." That particular ad lib was also the focal point of one of the first New York hip hop records to sample Lyn Collins: the 1987 single "Bad Sister" by Queens rapper Roxanne Shante.

Of course, the most famous use of "Think (About It)" came about in 1988, right at the height of New York hip hop's infatuation with James Brown breakbeats. The Harlem duo Rob Base & DJ E-Z Rock signed with Profile Records, one of the dominant rap labels of the '80s (Run-DMC, Dana Dane). Their first single for the label, "It Takes Two," featured Rob Base's charismatic rhymes – "I wanna rock right now" remains one of rap's greatest opening proclamations – over a generous sampling of "Think," kept at its original 112 BPM tempo.

Rob Base and DJ E-Z Rock were initially only interested in "Think" for its drums. "First, we picked out the breakbeat," Base told NPR in 2018. "But when I listened to the whole song, I was like, 'Yo, this song is dope.'" The "Yeah! Woo!" ad libs became a key part of "It Takes Two," along with the horns, guitars, and bass played by the J.B.'s, and a couple of lines of the Lyn Collins vocal, re-recorded by Rhonda Parris – "The record company wanted to bring in another singer to do it for copyright reasons or something like that."

"It Takes Two" took a few months to break out as a regional hit, but it eventually crossed over to the mainstream about as much as any hip hop song could in those days. It peaked at #36 on the Hot 100, and in 1989, the staff of *Spin* magazine boldly put the then-recent track at the top of their list of "The 100 Greatest Singles of All Time." "It Takes Two" was popular all over America, but we know it was particularly ubiquitous in Baltimore because of one the most famous books written about the city.

Baltimore Sun journalist David Simon spent the entirety of 1988 embedded within the Baltimore PD's homicide unit for the book *Homicide: A Year on the Killing Streets.* The summer of '88, one of the hottest on record at the time in Baltimore, is captured vividly by Simon in one of the book's most memorable passages, a sort of literary montage set to the beat of the most inescapable song of the year, "It Takes Two."

Like many of the brilliant drummers who made lasting contributions to popular music, Jabo Starks didn't receive a songwriting credit for "Think (About It)" or many other James Brown classics he played on (Brown and Rob Base are the only two credited writers on "It Takes Two"). Brown and his bands may have revolutionized rhythm in American pop, but songwriting in the '60s and '70s was still largely defined by more traditional compositional elements like lyrics, melodies, and chord structures. The way a drummer played a song could make or break a record, but that was still considered arranging, which, unlike songwriting, usually comes with no official credit or royalties – and, of course, many of the songs that sampled "Think" didn't even generate royalties for Brown, the putative sole author of the song.

The stark, hard-hitting drums of James Brown samples never entirely went away in hip hop, but after their late-'80s saturation point, beatmakers started turning towards the more maximalist funk of Parliament-Funkadelic or softer, more melodic loops from jazz records. In Baltimore, however, "Think (About It)" never went away, and its associations with Brown breakbeat mania and "It Takes Two" give club music an extra dimension of nostalgia – it conjures both the '70s, when it was recorded, and the late '80s, when it gained popularity as a sample.

Starks, who died in 2018, reflected on being one of the most sampled drummers of all time in a 2015 interview with *Mobile Bay Magazine*, and wished for a little more acknowledgment from the countless rappers, singers, and producers who looped his beats: "The least they could do is say where they got them from." If Starks knew of his impact on Baltimore music in particular, he never addressed it publicly. Nor did Collins, who died in 2005. Collins did, however, continue performing "Think," and the music from the two albums she recorded for People Records, for the rest of her life. She also occasionally recorded new songs, including some house music singles in the '90s, though they bore little resemblance to the Baltimore dance tracks that sampled her music the most.

The "Think" breakbeat didn't become a staple of Baltimore dance tracks until the early '90s, a couple of years after "It Takes Two" hit the pop charts. But when the break took over Baltimore, the tempo was picked up to a more frenetic pace, usually somewhere between 124 and 130 BPM, and the focus was almost entirely on the drums and tambourine – and sometimes that "Ya bad, sister!" ad lib. As slicker forms of house music moved towards the mainstream, largely with synthetic drum sounds and rigidly quantized drum machine patterns, Baltimore producers moved in the opposite direction, doubling down on samples of real drummers, leading many to dub the sound "Baltimore breaks" or "Baltimore breakbeat" before "Baltimore club" became the more universally recognized name for the genre.

The only track that competes with "Think (About It)" for its sheer ubiquity in Baltimore club music is Gaz's "Sing Sing." The Pan-European disco group Gaz only released one self-titled album, recorded in Munich, Germany, in 1978. Thor Baldursson from Iceland, a keyboardist and arranger who'd worked on genre-defining disco hits with Donna Summer and Giorgio Moroder, formed Gaz with a Swede, Mats Bjorklund, and a German, Jurgen S. Korduletsch.

Gaz was released by the influential New York–based dance label Salsoul Records, and a promotional sheet included in copies of the album sent to radio stations features a sentence about each song. "Sing Sing" is described as a "late night peak record for your slower tempo part of the evening." *Gaz* didn't make major ripples on the charts, even in '78, when just about everything disco was moving units. But by the early '80s, "Sing Sing" became a minor classic among DJs, sampled by Grandmaster Flash and looped on the fourth volume of *Ultimate Beats and Breaks.*

Where "Think (About It)" was a spare and gritty funk track that emanates an effortless cool beyond the most sampled sections, listening to all seven minutes of the original "Sing Sing" can be a little jarring if you're primarily familiar with it via breakbeats. It's a lush, sugary disco confection with male and female vocals, chicken-scratch guitar, synths, and saxophone. The first widely sampled section of the song arrives at three minutes and 48 seconds, more than halfway into the song, when the bridge strips the rhythm track down to its basic elements: drums, handclaps with a heavy echo, minimal stabs of bass guitar, shaker percussion, and what seems to be a human mouth imitating shakers with "chka chka" sounds. From there, the song keeps swapping elements in and out, with several distinct sections that have been sampled countless times, often by hip hop artists like Wu-Tang Clan and Lil Jon.

"Everything is in there," DJ Technics said in a 2014 interview with Red Bull Music Academy. "It's not like the 'Amen' [break] where you only got three seconds to work with. In 'Sing Sing,' it's four or five minutes of them jamming out and the pattern changes three or four times. EQ it different and it's gonna sound different in every song you use it in. People know that break and it sounds good in everything." The original "Sing Sing" cruises along at 114 BPM, once again sped up slightly by Baltimore producers to 124 to 130 BPM, taking on a certain frenzied urgency in the process.

At some point, Baltimore producers developed a love/hate relationship with how much better "Sing Sing" and "Think (About It)" worked than any other breakbeats they used. These guys spent years digging in the crates, amassing massive vinyl collections and searching for rare grooves, but much of what they found either wouldn't work in Baltimore clubs, or would only work in combination with one or both of those two breaks. "We had conversations about it, like, man, we gotta get rid of this 'Sing Sing,' we can't keep puttin' this in everything," Booman remembers with a laugh.

"They became standard once we tried to deviate from them and we saw that things didn't work," K.W. Griff says. "And then we'd put it back in, and be like, 'Yup, that's what it needed, it's gotta stay.'" In 2013, Salsoul Records sued

Australian dance pop star Kylie Minogue and Warner Bros. for sampling "Sing Sing" on the 2007 song "Speakerphone." Fortunately, Salsoul has never been so litigious with the small independent dance labels that have made "Sing Sing" into a dancefloor staple.

Ultimately, Baltimore producers had to work to be more creative to put fresh new spins on "Think" and "Sing Sing," often combining them with each other and other breaks from the '60s or '70s to great effect. "Everybody had the same records for the most part," Booman says. "The main thing was, 'How good could you flip it?' Our thing, we would take some little weird sound, or a different way to chop something up, to try to make it a little different."

Chapter 4
Party People

Scottie B. made his transition from spinning at house parties to working in clubs when his cousin got him a doorman job at the Body Factory on Reisterstown Road, which he parlayed into a DJ slot. "They wanted me to play house, and I wasn't," he says, recalling that at that point he still preferred B-boy breakbeats to four-on-the-floor Chicago tracks. "I was playing 'Sing Sing,' 'Dance to the Drummer's Beat,' 'Funk Box,' Baltimore party classics you would always play. You would play that two or three times a night." It was at the Body Factory that Scottie B. met DJ Technics, who'd become one of his label's first acts.

Baltimore's hip hop fans and house fans were just starting to agree on songs that appealed to both crowds, like Royal House's 1987 single "Party People." Royal House was an alias of legendary Brooklyn producer Todd Terry, and "Party People" was an early blueprint for what would come to be known in the late '80s as "hip house." The track opened with the clarion call "Gotta have house music!" from Marshall Jefferson's 1986 Chicago house anthem "Move Your Body," followed by more vocal samples from two divergent strains of hip hop: Afrika Bambaataa's electro classic "Planet Rock" and T-La Rock's "It's Yours," the early Def Jam single that epitomized Rick Rubin's brand of hard-hitting minimalism.

Scottie B. can still vividly recall a conversation at the Body Factory regarding "Party People" that tipped him to the potential of this alchemy:

> "I was in the bathroom. One of my friends came in there and says, 'Yo, I like house music, I'm startin' to like that stuff y'all playin', but it's this one record. It was like a house record with fuckin' Run-DMC [sic] samples in it.' And when he said that, I was like, 'This shit's gonna start getting big.'"

"The music started crossing, and people realized it," Scottie B. says. "House music was just starting to touch that yo crowd. It wasn't even touchin' 'em yet, but it was on the precipice of doin' it." He cites a 1987 classic by Chicago producer Ralphi Rosario as the moment that the dam between the two scenes really broke and Baltimore's hip hop faithful fully embraced dance beats. "The first big house record for the yo crowd was 'You Used to Hold Me.'"

Soon, Baltimore dancefloors developed a tendency to gravitate towards records that didn't resonate elsewhere. Perhaps it's a simple quirk of local taste, or how Baltimore differed regionally or demographically from other dance music hotbeds as a Black working-class East Coast city, existing outside of the immediate influence of New York's powerful DJs and media outlets. Rhythm Warfare's breakbeat-driven track "Two Notches (The War Call)" and Double Impact's thumping Euro house track "My House" wound up in the record store "cutout" bins in other cities, sold for a fraction of the original sticker price. "The labels would tell you, 'Oh, Rhythm Warfare, big in Baltimore, total flop for us. Double Impact, huge in Baltimore, total flop for us, all those records were cutouts,'" Scottie B. remembers with a laugh.

"In Baltimore, you know, it's funny, because even nowadays, the hip hop DJs, they play house, it's always been like that," Scottie B. says. "Baltimore DJs had to play everything, even way back."

Hip house had more cultural currency in the UK, where rave culture was becoming a popular phenomenon and excitable weekly music magazines were always on the prowl for new genres to hype up. "Rok da House," by the production team Beatmasters and the rap duo Cookie Crew, both from London, was widely hailed as the first hip house song. It was a top-5 hit in the UK in early 1988, but missed the charts in America.

American rap fans mostly knew hip house via a parody of the genre by the New York group the Jungle Brothers, members of the progressive Native Tongues collective. "I'll House You" was based on another Royal House track by Todd Terry, "Can You Party." Released as a non-album single, it became the Jungle Brothers' first radio hit, reaching #16 on Billboard's Hot Rap Songs chart, and was appended to latter pressings of their classic 1988 debut *Straight Out the Jungle*.

Three years later, their Native Tongues associates De La Soul kept the joke going with a song called "Kicked Out the House," which opened with Trugoy the Dove's disclaimer: "In no way are we trying to disrespect any sort of house or club music, but we're just glad that we're not doing it." The whimsical album track is accidentally significant in the sense that it's the first notable on-record reference to "club music" as a synonym for house music or a broader umbrella term for any kind of music people dance to in a club. "Club music" was a common colloquialism in Baltimore years before "Baltimore club music" was formally recognized as a genre, but the De La Soul track was evidence that the phrase "club music" was common enough up and down the East Coast that a New York group was using it back in 1991.

Scottie B. and Shawn Caesar, who'd forge one of the most enduring and consequential partnerships in Baltimore club music, met in 1989 through a mutual association with the Baltimore rapper King D, and became fast friends. "They were doing these talent show things, and [Shawn] was DJing for a rapper that I used to DJ for," Scottie B. recalls.

"Shawn had seen me around because I'm a little older than him, he'd seen me DJing some place while he was comin' up, but he was new to me. We just cliqued out with each other and was hangin' out that day and switched numbers, and then that was it," Scottie B. says. Soon, they were a tight pair. "Me and Shawn was like every day with each other, I don't even know how that happened."

With Odell's in decline, other clubs were on the rise in Baltimore. The Famous Ballroom on Charles Street, the same place that had hosted jazz legends like John Coltrane in the '60s, became Godfrey's Famous Ballroom in 1986, and began hosting DJ nights as well as concerts. Wayne Davis, who'd left Odell's after its first raid by federal agents, became a partner in Club Fantasy at 600 N. Howard Street, his first time running a club of his own, in 1988.

"It was pretty much a house, all cut up and chopped up," Davis says of Fantasy, which likely took its name from "Fantasy," the 1984 Z-Factor and Jesse Saunders track that has been called the first house record. "I went and had to take down some non-structural walls to open the space up, we utilized three floors. The first floor was the lobby, and they had a restaurant down there and coat check. Then the second floor was the main dance area, and the third floor, we had pool tables and stuff like that up there. So we were able to hold about three hundred people."

Like Odell's, Fantasy didn't have a liquor license. "We sold sodas and non-alcoholic beverages. We'd have a keg of beer and we'd give away beer and nobody ever messed with us about that," Davis says. Also like Odell's, Fantasy catered to different people on different nights of the week. "The Friday crowd was kind of our college crowd. Our Saturday crowd was the house music crowd. At Fantasy the gay crowd came predominantly on a Sunday night."

"Shawn played at Fantasy, I played Godfrey's," Scottie B. says. "I had the real gruff street crowd, he had the college kids. And when the college kids wanted a little adventure they'd come up to Godfrey's. And when the Godfrey's kids wanted to hear a little more house than I could give them, they'd go holla at Shawn on Friday."

"The first major club that I DJed in was Godfrey's one night," remembers DJ Kool Breez, who wasn't even old enough to drive yet in 1989. "That was the first time I really mixed in a spot that I'm like, 'Oh shit, I'm at Godfrey's and I'm on the turntables.' It was mind blowin'."

One night at Fantasy, Scottie B. was in Caesar's DJ booth, egging his friend on to throw a rap song into his house set. "I said, 'Play it now! You can get away with it – I'm tellin' you!' So he started playing hip hop and the crowd went crazy," Scottie B. recalled to the *Baltimore Sun* in 2016.

The owner of the club was not pleased, according to Caesar: "Wayne came in the booth [and said], 'Shawn, what are you doing?!'"

"It was a couple songs where they would get really riled up and start fightin' and carryin' on. And I would ask them not to play that, but that was only for that reason," says Davis.

Chapter 5
Doo Doo Brown

While hip house was a relatively short-lived blip in popular music outside the UK, the fusion of rap and dance music that really made waves in America was Miami bass, also known as booty bass. Groups like 2 Live Crew spit hypersexual rhymes over fast beats with heavy low end, programmed on the Roland TR-808 drum machine. Senate hearings on explicit lyrical content in popular rock and R&B songs had already been headline news in 1985. And with the 1986 album *The 2 Live Crew Is What We Are,* featuring songs like "Throw the D" and "We Want Some Pussy," 2 Live Crew and their frontman, Luther "Uncle Luke" Campbell, stepped eagerly into the culture war, thumbing their noses at the Parents Music Resource Center, a pro-censorship organization co-founded by Senator Al Gore's wife Tipper.

Some musicians who write about sex and love might resent their artistic expression being likened to pornography, but 2 Live Crew were proudly pornographic, even sampling audio from adult films. Every time a politician denounced 2 Live Crew or a record store clerk was charged with felony corruption of a minor for selling their album to a teenager, the group got more popular. By 1989, 2 Live Crew had a top-40 single, "Me So Horny," and their third album, *As Nasty as They Wanna Be*, became the first southern rap album to sell a million copies.

Despite a preference for breakbeats over 808s, Baltimore crowds and Baltimore DJs had a clear affinity for the raw and lewd sound of Miami bass, and it became a recognizable influence on what would become Baltimore club music. The follow-up single to "Me So Horny" was "C'mon Babe," which featured 2 Live Crew rapper Brother Marquis declaring, "Lick my ass up and down / Lick it 'til your tongue turns doo doo brown."

Before DJ Equalizer had formally launched the Inner City Records Co. label, he was selling white label 12"s out of his store, and one of his most popular tracks was a 1989 edit of "C'Mon Babe" that looped the "doo doo brown" section. "You couldn't keep up with the pressings or nothin', it just blew up that bad," Equalizer remembers. And one of the people who took notice of the white label's popularity was one of Baltimore radio's biggest stars, Frank Ski.

Frank Rodriguez, was born in Harlem in 1964, grew up in Miami, and moved to Washington, D.C., to attend the University of the District of Columbia and work as a paralegal in the '80s. As Frank Ski, he began his radio career on the campus radio station WUDC with one of the region's first hip hop programs, *Breakers Delight*. In 1985, Frank Ski began working night shifts at Baltimore's V103 (WXYV), and eventually became one of the station's most popular on-air personalities, hosting "Frank and Jean in the Morning" with Jean Ross.

Frank Ski was among the first, if not the very first, to bring the sound that had been fomenting in Baltimore clubs onto mainstream radio airwaves. In 1991, he seized on the local popularity of Equalizer's edit of 2 Live Crew's "C'mon Babe," spinning it off into a whole new song called "Doo Doo Brown." The song was credited to 2 Hyped Brothers & A

Dog, a group that consisted of Frank Ski, Stanley Evans Jr., and, well, Frank's dog Rondo.

"Doo Doo Brown" featured samples of the "ya bad, sister" section of "Think (About It)" as well as old party-starting favorites like Afrika Bambaataa's "Planet Rock." On the track, Frank Ski and Evans delivered rudimentary but entertaining rhymes about Doo Doo Brown, now a character with his own theme song, whereas the phrase had been a puerile euphemism for analingus in the 2 Live Crew lyric. With V103 as Frank Ski's personal hype machine, "Doo Doo Brown" quickly became a hit in Baltimore, and then went national.

Frank Ski formed a label, Deco Records, and recorded a 2 Hyped Brothers album, *Ya Rollin' Doo Doo*. The distributor that helped get the album into stores across the country was the pioneering New York house and hip hop label Warlock Records, which had released Todd Terry's Royal House singles that'd had a powerful influence on Baltimore DJs a few years earlier.

Throughout the '90s, Miami bass tracks and Miami bass–influenced tracks would have a massive impact on the pop charts. Tag Team's 1993 single "Whoomp! (There It Is)" and the Quad City DJs' 1996 song "C'mon N' Ride It (The Train)" were both top 5 hits on the Hot 100. By that standard, "Doo Doo Brown" was a minor sensation, peaking at #90 on the Hot 100 and #65 on the R&B chart. "Doo Doo Brown" was very much part of the pop culture landscape in 1991, however, and the first dance or hip hop record of any kind from Baltimore that many people had ever heard, myself included. I was nine years old at the time. And while I would visit my father in Baltimore on weekends, I first heard kids on the school bus quoting "Doo Doo Brown" in Delaware, where I lived with my mother.

The "Doo Doo Brown" video got airplay on *Yo! MTV Raps*, then television's biggest showcase for hip hop. It was directed by a 24-year-old Maryland native named Chris Robinson, who'd go on to direct videos for rap superstars like Jay-Z and Lil Wayne, as well as the 2006 feature film *ATL*. The comedian Gordon Brown III adopted Doo Doo Brown as a nickname. His 1992 appearance on HBO's *Def Comedy Jam* ended with him pantomiming the act of eating a woman's ass and declaring, "They don't call me Doo Doo Brown for nothin'!"

Uncle Luke of 2 Live Crew appreciated what Frank Ski did with the "C'mon Babe" sample, and his 1992 solo album *I Got Shit on My Mind* opened with "I Wanna Rock," which riffed on the "doo doo brown" theme and also sampled Rob Base's voice from "It Takes Two." "I Wanna Rock" was a bigger chart hit than the 2 Hyped Brothers song, reaching #73 on the Hot 100. These days, someone requesting that a DJ play "Doo Doo Brown" could be referring to "C'mon Babe," "I Wanna Rock," or "Doo Doo Brown," depending on what part of the country you're in.

Equalizer wasn't directly involved in the 2 Hyped Brothers project, but took no umbrage at Frank Ski scoring big with a track he partly inspired. "When he was working on 'Doo Doo Brown,' I was busy in the studio producing other artists," Equalizer recalls. "Me and Frank have always been on friendly terms, y'know, I could call him at his house. We never had a problem, we always got along fine."

Soon after "Doo Doo Brown," the first official Inner City Records Co. 12" was released under Equalizer's alias, Sounds of Silence, featuring three songs that Equalizer and DJ Scottie B. created together (the latter credited as "D.J. Scotty B."). The three breakbeat-heavy songs ranged from 118 BPM to

130 BPM, evidence that Baltimore club had not yet settled into a uniform tempo. Both "All About Pussy" and "Much Too Much" featured 2 Live Crew–style samples of the enthusiastic moans of adult film actresses – the former also featured excerpts of a profane routine by Andrew "Dice" Clay, the massively popular New York comedian who was headlining arenas in the early '90s.

The slower and less risque lead track on the Equalizer and Scottie 12" "I Got the Rhythm" wound up being the biggest hit from the release. After all, it was the only one that wasn't too lewd for public broadcasting. "Next thing you know, Frank Ski was playing the living shit out of it on the radio," Equalizer says. "He was a tremendous promoter of music."

Chapter 6
My Crew Be Unruly

Not long after Scottie B. made his on-record debut with "I Got the Rhythm," Shawn Caesar made his first appearance on wax with "Booty Mission (Yo, Yo Where The Ho's At?)," a boom bap hip hop track released under the group name Runaway Slaves. The single was released by the well-funded but short-lived label Savage Records and distributed by BMG – Shawn Caesar was, however briefly, labelmates with David Bowie. A video for "Booty Mission" was produced, Caesar went on a promotional tour in the UK, and the 12" single featured a remix by Salaam Remi, who would begin producing mainstream hits for Ini Kamoze and the Fugees within a couple of years.

At the time, Scottie B. was working at Inner City Records, and Caesar was working at DJ's Outlet at Old Town Mall alongside Marc Henry and Sean Marshall. "We were battling to see who could sell more of the other's record," Caesar told the *Baltimore Sun* in 2016. "[Scottie] had a better record store situation than I did, so he sold more copies of my record than I sold of his."

Now that Caesar and Scottie B. had both gotten a taste of making a record and hearing their ideas on wax, they decided to team up. "I did one, then he did one, and then we were like, 'Alright, we're ready to do this together,'" Scottie B. says. At first, they branded themselves as the Underground

Trak Team, but soon they decided to start a label together, co-founding it with Baltimore house producer Christopher "Karizma" Clayton, born in 1970.

I'd interviewed Scottie B. numerous times over the last 18 years before it occurred to me one day, toward the end of working on this book, to ask Scottie who actually came up with the name of Unruly Records. I'd always assumed that the idea came from one of the label's three co-founders. To my surprise, he volunteered that the name came from a friend, Tierre Brownlee, with whom he frequently DJed in clubs at the time.

"Tierre used to say little catchphrases, he used to always say, 'Man, they're getting unruly in here,'" Scottie remembers. One day, Scottie B., Caesar, and Brownlee were hanging out, and began brainstorming for a label name. "We were sitting there, it was us three in my room, and we were like, 'We gotta come up with a name for this shit.' And then he just popped up like, 'Unruly motherfuckin' Records,' and we looked at each other like, 'That's it. That's it.'"

The day after Scottie told me that story, I had an interview scheduled with DJ Tie.Be. And until he began telling me the same story, I didn't realize that he was Tierre Brownlee, who went by DJ Tierre in the '90s. "We was up on Labyrinth Road, in the little apartment he had. He would make stuff in his little studio, that's where me, him, and Shawn sat on crates in his studio and Unruly was born," says Brownlee, born in 1972.

Brownlee's creativity and over-the-top personality also manifested in a quirky ritual he started while hanging out at the Inner City Records location on Howard Street with Scottie B. The track for the Baltimore Light Rail system, the public transit used by many commuters to get downtown, ran right past the front of the store. "I would DJ in the record store," Brownlee remembers. "If the record was hot, I'd go out there and touch the third rail. They'd be like, 'Yo, what you doin'?' I'm goin' out and touchin' the third rail because it's a hot record! You know what I'm sayin'? It was just somethin' that I did." (Please note that touching the third rail, which provides electricity to the trains, is extremely dangerous and not recommended.)

Brownlee DJed house music at Club Ozone with DJ Cornbread, warming up the crowd for Scottie B. Brownlee also made mixtapes and frequently played parties with DJ Paradise. But between a stint in the U.S. Army and getting a day job to provide for his family, Brownlee never devoted himself full time to music like his friends at Unruly Records, and he never released anything on the label he named. "When they started really pressing records, I was workin', I was nine to five. I love the music still, but I was a taxpayer, I was locked in, I had to take care of them kids, man, you know how that is," he says. "I'm not bashin' nobody, but I wish I woulda had paperwork to say who I was and what I did."

Initially, Unruly was conceived primarily as a vehicle for tracks by the founders of the label. "We wanted to put out our records at first," Scottie says. Pretty quickly, however, Unruly began releasing tracks by many of the scene's best producers, including DJ Class, DJ Technics, DJ Booman, and K.W. Griff.

Unruly averaged eight to ten releases a year, primarily 12" EPs with two or a handful of songs. And the label's brand eventually became strong enough that the Unruly name sometimes meant more than the individual artist or song on a Baltimore shop's wall display of new releases. "After a while, the label had a visual print, so people would go to the record store and they would see the black and yellow, and they were like, 'I wanna hear this,'" says Scottie B, adding that the color scheme was picked out by the more detail-oriented Caesar. "I didn't care. If it would've been me, it wouldn't have even had the label. I didn't even think about shit like that. He thinks about shit like that."

Unruly also began introducing sublabels, including Hardhead Records, heralded as "the son of Unruly" on 12" labels, which had its own color scheme. "[Hardhead] was the white label with the red lettering, so you would see a lot of those in record stores. Soon as you saw it on the wall you would just grab it, because you knew it was somethin' hot. And it was always either us or [DJ] Technics, or [DJ] Kool Breeze, or [DJ] Excel, [DJ Big] Red, Karizma," Griff remembers. DJ Excel, born in 1976, was still a teenager when he released "This DJ" and "Captain Jack" on a Hardhead 12" in 1995.

In 1995, the Baltimore rapper Sparrow released his debut single "Physics" on Unruly, a record that has become highly sought after by the international community of collectors of '90s underground hip hop. "That gets like five to eight hundred dollars a pop on vinyl now," Scottie B. says. Sparrow's list of thank-yous on the "Physics" 12" included Labtekwon, another underground Baltimore rapper who'd already begun building his prodigious catalog of self-released albums.

"We were thinking like Unruly was gonna be house and hip hop," Scottie B. says, with Hardhead created primarily for a third genre that didn't have a definite name yet, the music that would eventually be called Baltimore club. For a while, Unruly had its own Friday-night DJ block on V103, designed to showcase those three genres. "I played the club, Karizma played house, Shawn played hip hop, and we played an hour each."

Karizma made a few of the best early Unruly tracks, including "Kong" and "Mamakossa," but his direct involvement in running the label was relatively short-lived. Karizma was more connected to the global house music mainstream alongside the Basement Boys, which he joined in the mid-'90s, and he was soon in high demand as a DJ around the world, while the club music faction of Unruly stayed focused on the Baltimore market.

Tierre Brownlee speaks of Karizma with a sense of awe and respect in his voice. "True story, I see Karizma, and he just came from, I think he was in Australia or somewhere. And I see this motherfucker walkin' up Saratoga Street and he got Gucci flip-flops on. I'm like, yo! Because that's when he was doing shit with Pioneer, he was traveling, he was on tour, he was in Tokyo, all this kinda stuff. And I'm walkin' up Saratoga Street, and I'm like, is that fuckin' Karizma?"

With the other two founders left to guide Unruly for most of its history, Scottie B. and Shawn Caesar became one of Baltimore club's iconic duos. In a sense, Baltimore club's top label being run by one White man and one Black man was emblematic of how the scene was built by an interracial mix of DJs and producers. It also created a parallel to hip hop's most important label, Def Jam, and its founders, Rick Rubin and Russell Simmons.

The dynamic between the heads of Unruly ran counter to what one might expect given their respective races. Scottie B. spun more hip hop while Caesar leaned more towards house. Scottie B. was constantly active on the club scene and focused on the music, while Caesar was increasingly putting in office hours to run the label's day-to-day business. "It was kind of like a strategy: I would stay out there, and Shawn would stay in there," Scottie B. says.

"Scottie already had a reputation for playing for Black

crowds," Brownlee says, noting that some nights Scottie B. may have been the only White person in the club. "I ain't seen no [other] White people in the Ozone, unless they're the police and they was outside."

"Scottie took me to some places that I was like, 'Yo, I'm scared!' He's White, and *I'm* scared! 'Nah, they cool, yo, they cool,'" Brownlee says with a laugh. "He's a human being, that's my brother, and I love him. Scottie is who he is. If you wanna say 'hood pass,' Scottie had a pass before the pass was the pass."

In the wake of the success of "Doo Doo Brown," the song's title became a shorthand for the dance tracks coming out of Baltimore. "I remember at some point somebody callin' it 'doo dew music,' they were tryin' to give club a name," DJ Booman says. He, K.W. Griff, and Jimmy Jones released much of their music under the group name Doo Dew Kidz, which later became the name of their label. For years, songs that didn't even contain the 2 Live Crew sample had names like "Doo Dew Rock," which was a Dukeyman track that remixed Michael Jackson's "Rock with You."

"They used to call it 'knucklehead music,' then club music," DJ Patrick recalls. "The name started changing, because it wasn't gettin' no radio play, it was all in the club." In 1996, DJ Technics created an Unruly sublabel called Knucklehead Records, which would release music by Dukeyman, Rod Lee, Karizma, Jimmy Jones, DJ Boobie, and others. Music Liberated owner Bernie Rabinowitz had a label called Baltimore Breakbeat Records, and Baltimore breakbeat and Baltimore breaks were widely used names for the genre for years – even the Philadelphia store 611 Records had a vinyl bin labeled "Baltimore breaks" in the '90s.

Liaison Records, based in Laurel, Maryland, distributed a

number of Baltimore club labels, including Unruly, Inner City, and Deco. DJ Equalizer remembers a fateful conversation with the distributor when he was releasing a best-of EP in the mid-'90s. "Tom Goldfogle from Liaison, he gave me a call. And he's like, 'Bob, look, y'know, I keep getting these calls from overseas, they wanna know where they can hear more of that Baltimore club music.' That right there is the moment that God made club music, that was the exact moment."

Chapter 7
The Paradox

Both Fantasy and Godfrey's closed down in the early '90s. Godfrey's had been neighbors with a movie theater, the Charles Theatre, and eventually the space that housed Godfrey's became part of an expansion of the Charles.

Because Fantasy was essentially a converted rowhouse in a residential area, it was shut down by city government, which became a learning experience for Wayne Davis. "That was my first time as a partner with ownership. The [co-owner] had the place already set up, with me not knowing what type of licensing was required," he says. "We were forced out of the city because of the complaints they were getting about the music [volume] level. They started messing with us, and eventually found in the zoning that the permitted use was not what we were using the building as."

In 1991, Wayne Davis opened the Paradox in a warehouse space at 1310 Russell Street, which would become arguably the definitive Baltimore dance club over the next 25 years. More conventional house music thrived at the Paradox, particularly Scott Henry and Charles Feelgood's long-running Thursday-night party, Fever. But on the weekends it was the place where homegrown Baltimore club tracks became the local classics that DJs still play to this day.

Davis kept an open mind, to a point, about the newer, more aggressive sounds that those DJs brought into the Paradox, increasingly tracks they'd produced themselves. If nothing else, Davis understood that it was what people were coming to his club to hear. "My roots were more with what evolved into house music. The hip hop and the Baltimore club music was not anything that I was attracted to, but it was [popular] for the crowd, so I dealt with it in that perspective. I wasn't that much involved in the creativity of it," he says.

The Paradox, a 13,000-square-foot concrete box, was far more spacious than the 300-capacity Fantasy. "Our legal capacity of the Paradox was really like 800 or something, but we've had way more, and it was still comfortable with a thousand people in there. When you would start getting over 1200, then it would start getting a little crowded," Davis says.

Davis came up with the name of the Paradox as a reference to the contrast between the club's anonymous industrial exterior and the lively nights of music that took place inside it. "I'd read what a paradox was and I thought of the warehouse, it looked like an empty warehouse and you go in and it's a club," he says. "And then I liked the sound of it. I was thinking of something that would have a ring to it."

With the experience of Fantasy's shutdown fresh in his mind, Davis made smarter decisions from the beginning to ensure the Paradox's longevity. "I learned from that to make sure that when I went to open the Paradox, I played the game, gettin' all my proper paperwork and stuff like that," he says. "When I went to the zoning board, I told them what my intended use for the building was, and I was told this would be sufficient to do what I want to do. Then a storage place down in the Camden Yards area around the corner from us started complaining about the crowds and stuff. So we had to have a hearing, and as a result of the hearing, we came out stronger than we went in, we were granted a legal after-hours [operating license]."

Like its predecessors, the Paradox had no liquor license. "It was like a BYOB situation until they passed a law stating 'no BYOB,'" Davis says. "But we never got in any trouble with the liquor board."

Paradox's legendary sound system was built up and refined over a few years. "At Paradox we started with getting cabinets from a place in Wheaton, Maryland, called Washington Pro Sound," Davis says. "We started building a system, just kinda do-it-yourself with my knowledge of what equipment, what type of speakers, based on what I learned from the Richard Long sound system." Long, who'd designed the Odell's sound system, had died of AIDS in 1986.

"As a DJ myself, my pet peeve was sound [quality]," Davis says. "So that made me, when I was doing my club, try to make sure the sound [was right], and it was not so much for loudness but for clarity. So even though our system was able to be played extremely loud, most of the time I would try to forbid that, because it wasn't necessary for it to be that loud to be enjoyable."

The sound engineer Dave Soto, who'd done the sound system for Club Shelter in New York, eventually redid the Paradox system and helped it reach its full power. "They built the club around the kids as we danced week after week," Ultra Nate told the *Baltimore Sun* in 2016.

"I've been to many clubs throughout the East Coast; it definitely has one of the best sound systems that I've ever played on, outside of maybe Japan," DJ Oji told the *Sun* in the same article.

"The Paradox, it was a fuckin' mecca to me. People talk about the Tunnel in New York, stuff like that, the Paradox was that to me," says Tierre Brownlee. "If you ever experienced that sound system, you could be outside and feel the bass from outside, it was almost like the building was comin' apart. The lights would be blinkin' because the system was so pure."

"[Today] you see people go out and buy thousand-dollar outfits to go party for two hours," Brownlee continues. "We didn't do that. We dressed to sweat. We're not comin' to take pictures, we didn't worry about who the DJ was, we just worried about them playing that good music."

Chicago's second wave of house music, with its pumping beats and deadpan vocals, had a powerful effect on Baltimore dancefloors, particularly I-ROC-T's 1989 hit "Work Your Body (Mike's Houze Mixx)" and Cajmere's 1992 classic "Percolator." Those songs, perhaps more than any other songs made outside Baltimore, are honorary entries in the Baltimore club canon, staying in DJs' sets for years and influencing the insistent, minimalist tracks local producers would make in the '90s.

Baltimore producers were also innovating and creating sounds that would be sampled and imitated for years to come. DJ Technics created the hugely influential kick-drum pattern for the song "Dickontrol" – a simple variation on the classic "four-on-the-floor" pulse with triplet kicks at the end of the bar that would become the heartbeat of Baltimore club and several other styles of dance music.

DJ Rod Braxton, one of the most important DJs in '90s Baltimore club who wasn't also a producer, had a reel-to-reel tape deck in the booth to play unreleased music from local producers, sometimes months or years before it made it to vinyl. "The Paradox was bananas, college night was bananas, because Rod had the reel and he was getting' that fresh Doo Dew Kidz music," Tierre Brownlee remembers.

Braxton also had some signature blends that were never commercially released, like a "Ya Bad Sister" loop with the Barbara Tucker vocal from Hardrive's New York house classic "Deep Inside." "He merged 'em together for about five minutes, and that was a track, and it *banged* at the Paradox," K.W. Griff remembers.

"I remember me and Technics and Rod Braxton and Big Red, we did Christmas night '95 in the front room, and that shit was just off the hook," DJ Kool Breez says, naming one of his favorite nights at the Paradox.

Paradox was perhaps the most important piece of an emerging club music ecosystem in the '90s that included clubs like Louie Louie's and Club Choices, which was the same building that had previously been the Carousel and Gatsby's. Hammerjacks, a downtown brewery building converted into a venue on 1101 S. Howard Street, built a reputation as Baltimore's most legendary rock club in the '80s, booking hard rock bands like Guns N' Roses and Ratt. In the '90s, Hammerjacks also hosted dance nights and became one of the primary stomping grounds for Baltimore club. Hammerjacks closed in 1997, and reopened in 2000 on Guilford Avenue, where it remained a vital part of the club music scene. The Shake & Bake Family Fun Center on Pennsylvania Avenue, an all-ages space with a skating rink and a bowling alley, became part of the circuit for Baltimore club DJs.

According to Scottie B., there wasn't a substantial difference in the crowds at these different venues in the '90s, or in what club records they wanted to hear. "It was all the same at one point," he says. "If you went to Shake & Bake or you went to Ozone or Hammerjacks, I mean they were all basically the same kind of people, same profile. They was in there to hear that stuff."

Brownlee remembers some distinctions between different crowds, though. "I would leave from Ozone and go to the Paradox on Saturday. I would go from the knucklehead crowd, we used to call 'em that, and go down there to Saturdays at the Paradox with the melting pot," Brownlee says. "Now don't get me wrong, you could get your ass whooped at the Paradox on Friday night. Friday was college night, so it was more HBCUs [historically Black colleges and universities]. But it wasn't that vibe on Saturday night."

Paradox's weekly schedule was a slight update of what Davis had done at Fantasy. "What dictates your crowd is the music. So each night, the music was totally different," Davis says. "We went down to Paradox with the already established night of the Friday night being the college crowd, and then the Saturday night was our house music crowd; we only started out with those two nights." Some Saturdays were also "industry nights" with featured performers, including Barbara Tucker herself.

"As people were exposed to the space, other promoters came. And that's when we started doing the Fever party, which was, well, now it's called EDM, but they were calling it a rave-type party or something like that, and that was every other Thursday," Davis says. "And then eventually the gay crowd kinda mingled with the house music, mixed, diverse crowd. The Friday crowd was pretty much predominantly the Black Baltimore urban crowd. And then the rave crowd, y'know, was predominantly White."

One straight male producer once told me that club music was sometimes described by people as "faggy music," suggesting that despite the genre's unusually diverse audience in Baltimore, there was still some lingering homophobic stigma to house music.

Baltimore club music was also starting to find a younger and younger audience that heard it on the radio and wanted to dance to it in clubs like the Paradox, and who would become a bigger and bigger segment of the genre's audience over the next couple of decades. "Frank Ski brought in the teen crowd on Sunday afternoon, and it was all under-18 people," Davis says. "He had started it over at Hammerjacks, and then when they were closed, he brought it over there to me."

"Back then, the Black clubs that played club music were 16 and up. Hammerjacks, Godfrey's, Ozone," Scottie B. told *True Laurels* in 2014. "The music was fresh and people came out specifically for that music. That's what sparked the clubs having nights for younger people. Older people would party with younger people because the scene was so vibrant. You had 23–25-year-olds partying with younger kids in spots without alcohol because it was that hot. It was about dancing all night."

"Security on Friday nights, it got unruly. It got unruly down there," Brownlee says, not referencing the label but simply using one of his favorite words. "Bodies was flying, oh my goodness, man. Them dudes would grab people and throw 'em down the steps. Them wooden steps on the side right there? It was beautiful, fuckin' beautiful, I tell you. It was a work of art. You know what I mean? You ever seen somebody get fucked up and you be like, 'Goddamn, that's an art! This is a fuckin' piece of work to see how he took this guy apart!' It was amazing how they would grab three or four guys and just throw 'em down steps and police would be right outside waiting for 'em. I wanted to buy the steps on the side of the Paradox because of how many bodies flew down."

It was a different story at some of the rougher clubs, where fights breaking out was accepted as an inevitability. "On the other hand, at Ozone, security would get out the way. One time the security did try to fight dudes, and dudes knocked the speakers down on 'em," Brownlee says. "I don't understand why you would have a pool table in a club for hoodlums. So you know what was goin' on, then they was takin' pool balls and puttin' 'em in socks, swingin' 'em at people!"

Around the holidays, even the seasonal decorations became props in the fights at Ozone. "They had a fuckin' Christmas tree. They would throw people through the Christmas tree at one side, and dudes grab 'em on the other side and whoop they ass," Brownlee says. "And Scottie would be up in the booth, 'Security! Security! Turn the lights on!'"

Even as chaos might swirl around the DJ booth, however, the DJs themselves were afforded enough respect to remain untouched by violence in the clubs. "We was the DJs for the hood, and people took care of the DJs for the hood. We was, what you call it, made men," Brownlee says. "The street dudes told us to stay out of the street, 'Y'all keep on doin' what y'all doin', and playin' y'all music and mindin' y'all business, and we will do what we do on this side.'"

Chapter 8
Tony's Bitch Track

In 1992, Frank Ski was riding high on the success of "Doo Doo Brown," and Luther "Uncle Luke" Campbell, who appreciated seeing 2 Live Crew sampled and celebrated by an artist from another region, became an ally and collaborator. Frank Ski was hired to do official remixes for some of Luke's singles, including "Work It Out" and "It's My Birthday," and they began a string of collaborations.

Frank Ski started moving on from the 2 Hyped Brothers & A Dog name and rebranded, releasing the 1992 single "Hotel Money" with the artist billed as "Doo Doo Brown (formerly 2 Hyped Brothers & A Dog)." The next Deco Records single would be credited simply to Frank Ski, featuring two tracks that have arguably had a longer life in Baltimore clubs than "Doo Doo Brown."

The "Tony's Bitch Track"/"Whores in This House" single was released both on 12" vinyl and a cassette single, or "cassingle," a sign that Frank Ski had truly broken through to the music-buying public and wasn't primarily selling music to fellow DJs like other Baltimore club labels. The A-side was a star-making moment for one of the most memorable performers in Baltimore history.

Anthony "Miss Tony" Boston, born in 1967, was a fixture in the clubs in the late '80s and early '90s, running with a large group of friends and leading chants in the club. Miss

Tony made a more subdued appearance on a track on the *Ya Rollin' Doo Doo* album, "Fashion Police." But it was regular appearances on Frank Ski's radio show and "Tony's Bitch Track," which featured rants about his "PhD in dickology" and Tony promising "Bitch, I'll take your boyfriend," that made Miss Tony a star. Like most Baltimore club vocalists, Miss Tony didn't perform his vocals like a conventional singer, but in a couple of fleeting melodic runs with impressively controlled vibrato; on "Tony's Bitch Track," he hinted at the raw talent beneath the comical persona. The track kicked off a string of Miss Tony club classics that included "Whatzup Whatzup? (How You Wanna Carry It)" and "EA EA."

Anthony Boston grew up in Sandtown, the same working-class West Baltimore neighborhood that had decades earlier been home to Cab Calloway, Billie Holiday, and Thurgood Marshall. "As a kid, he was singing and dancing all the time. He even took dancing lessons," his brother Jermaine Boston told the *Baltimore Sun* in 2003. An openly gay drag performer, Anthony Boston became Miss Tony, flamboyantly holding court in a wig and a dress in local clubs. Boston first caught Frank Ski's eye at Shake & Bake, and he soon made Miss Tony the MC at his events and then a part of his morning show team.

One of Miss Tony's more ribald routines was to point out men in the club that he'd been with or was attracted to, something that could provoke anger among the homophobic or closeted. "'That's my baby father right there,' he would holler people names!" recalls Tierre Brownlee. Sometimes, things got out of hand. "One night someone tried to run Tony over in front of the Paradox on Saturday night," Brownlee says.

Fortunately, Boston was big enough and tough enough to handle the intolerance he sometimes faced in Baltimore – he worked security for the Housing Authority of Baltimore City in some of the most infamous projects in West Baltimore. "Tony was a security guard in Murphy Homes projects, Tony was a security guard in Lexington Terrace," Brownlee says.

The B-side of "Tony's Bitch Track" was another major club hit with a different vocalist. Frank Ski put together "Whores in This House" with Al "T" McLaran, a Warlock Records A&R man and a friend of Stanley Evans of 2 Hyped Brothers & A Dog. McLaran had first come down to Baltimore from New York to help finish the *Ya Rollin' Doo Doo* album. McLaran was a Brooklyn native who had been an MC with the early hip hop crew Jam On Productions, spent a couple of years in the United States Army, and released the rap single "Drunk Driving" on MCA in 1984 under the name Tuga.

Arnie Geher had just begun recording local bands at High Heel Studios in the Remington neighborhood in North Baltimore in 1990, a year or two before Frank Ski began recording there. Frank Ski conceived "Whores in This House" as sort of a hybrid of several other songs that were already popular in clubs. It had elements of "Greeks in the House," a song on *Ya Rollin' Doo Doo* saluting Black frats and sororities, as well as "Booty Mission (Yo, Yo Where the Ho's At)," Shawn Caesar's then-recent debut with Runaway Slaves. And the chorus was a play on the UK dance hit "Ghosties" by Zone, which sampled R. Dean Taylor's '60s R&B track "There's a Ghost in My House."

McLaran hadn't been a drill sergeant in his military years, but Frank Ski asked him to do his best "drill sergeant voice" to holler the song's title phrase. "I was known for my voice in the Army, because even when I wasn't supposed to be calling cadences, they pulled me out of formation to do it," McLaran says. Most of the track was programmed and performed by

McLaran at the direction of Frank Ski, who contributed some backing vocals.

For McLaran, it was just another day of work, but he started to suspect that they had a hit on their hands later that night, when they blasted the song in a parking lot near High Heel Studios (which still operates today as Wright Way Studios). "Some kids heard it, they lost their minds and started dancing like fools. I figured what the hell, it might work after all," McLaran remembers with a laugh.

The two producers initially agreed to release the 12" under the title *Frank Ski and Al T's Club Trax,* and McLaran was going to be Frank Ski's partner in Deco Records, so he only took a small cash payment for his work in the studio. Ultimately, though, that partnership never really panned out, and the 12" was billed as *Frank Ski's Club Trax*, to McLaran's chagrin. Frank Ski was listed as the sole producer and writer of "Whores," with McLaran only credited for the "vocal sample." This would lead to complications in the decades ahead as "Whores in This House" became one of the most sampled songs ever to come out of Baltimore, with McLaran's voice eventually appearing on a worldwide #1 hit.

Dwayne "Diamond K" Williams, born in 1974, was an aspiring teenage rapper in the early '90s. The first acquaintance he made who was already established in the local house and hip hop scenes was Ron "Dukeyman" Hall Jr. born on July 4, 1973. "Dukeyman and I met in '92. And we dated sisters, and that's how I met him," Diamond K recalls. "My first girlfriend was the younger sister of a girl he was dating, and he's at her house, and we're playing Uno. And like, he's got flashy jewelry, he's got clothes better than mine. I was thinking maybe he's a street guy, something like that. But he was like, 'No,' he was a barber, but he also did some music.

And he had a record at this time, he was in a group with DJ PreCise, they had a nice little underground buzz."

At 19 years old, Diamond K took a bold step toward entering the music industry when he sent Frank Ski, arguably the biggest recording artist and the biggest radio personality in Baltimore at the time, a demo for a song he'd written called "Where's Ya Boyfriend At." "He liked it, we met up, and we re-recorded it in a studio session. Miss Tony and Reggie Reg were there, they were all working on a project," Diamond K says. "I signed to Frank's label, that's how my path began in Baltimore club music."

Most of the aspiring rappers in Baltimore at the time, including Diamond K's friends, aspired to make the kind of hard, street-oriented hip hop that was popular in New York. But Diamond K felt an affinity for the more playful uptempo version of hip hop that 2 Live Crew and Frank Ski were making. "The guys that I was working with prior to meeting Frank, they were strictly hip hop–type folks, and they completely rejected this path," he says. "But I started touring with Miss Tony and I started to see that this was a good lane for me." "Where's Ya Boyfriend At" appeared on *Frank Ski's Club Trax – Volume 3* alongside Miss Tony's "Pull Ya Gunz Out" and "Bitch Track 2 – Yes!" as well as a remix of "Whores in This House."

Baltimore was perhaps slightly more accustomed to outrageously flamboyant drag performers than other places might have been at the time, given that one of the city's most recognizable counterculture figures had been Divine, the drag queen who starred in several John Waters films before dying in 1988. But in the early '90s, when RuPaul was only just beginning to become the first drag queen on the pop charts, meeting Miss Tony could be a culture shock for some in the Baltimore club scene. "He's, like, a six-foot guy, he's 300 pounds. And when I met him in '93, it's the hair, it's the nails, it's the whole thing, and I'd never seen anything like that before," Diamond K says. "But we did a lot of shows together, I opened up for him more times than I can remember in different cities. And he was just a cool person, we developed a friendship."

Before Baltimore club became popular throughout Maryland and surrounding states, another sound born in Washington, D.C., had dominated the region. Go-go music, a subgenre of funk that thrived in D.C. nightclubs and was widely disseminated on bootleg live recordings, had been locally popular since the '70s, occasionally bursting onto the pop charts with crossover hits like Chuck Brown's 1979 single "Bustin' Loose" and EU's 1988 single "Da Butt." The slow, loose live grooves of go-go and the fast, programmed beats of Baltimore club were very different styles, but they had a common ancestor in the music of James Brown, and they both had primarily Black audiences in the same area. They were in some ways too different to compete with each other directly, but both genres took a lot of oxygen away from local hip hop scenes in D.C. and Baltimore.

The eastern shore of Maryland, a cluster of rural towns and cities on the other side of the Chesapeake Bay near the Delaware border, was a secondary market for Baltimore and D.C. acts. And when Miss Tony and Diamond K took a trip down to the area, they found it was far more receptive to go-go than Baltimore club. "We were with a go-go band, I wanna say Backyard Band," Diamond K remembers. "I opened, and Tony came on, and they were excited for me, they were very excited for Tony. And then the go-go band came on, and they lost it, like I had never seen, like they were superstars. And I was like, 'This would not be this way in Baltimore.'"

Even if he was upstaged by the go-go band, Miss Tony still got some groupie love after the show. "I had a girlfriend at this time. So I'm in the hotel room, talking to her on the phone, you know what I mean, like the whole groupie thing wasn't even registering for me," Diamond K says. "But Tony, his room was next to mine, and Tony just had all these guys in and out of his room, in and out of his room," he laughs. "And I'm saying these are *guys*, you would look at him like, 'Oh, this is like a thug,' I got the airquotes, 'thug.'"

Frank Ski ran a tight ship with the acts on Deco Records, turning his protégés into local celebrities, deciding how to release their songs and when they would perform live. "What he had explained to me previously was, y'know, 'I'll do your booking. People are gonna call you up and try to book you. Push them to me, I'll be the bad guy and tell them the price that we need to be, because you don't need to do any shows in the city under a certain amount.'"

After a year with Deco, Diamond K gave in to the temptation to take one of the smaller local bookings that Frank Ski warned him against. "I was really really close with Scottie B. at this time," Diamond K remembers. "Scottie was DJing at a venue, and the promoter reached out and said they wanna get somebody on there, and I had the 'Boyfriend' record at the time."

Frank Ski set a price for a Diamond K performance that the promoter was not willing to pay, but Scottie B. went directly to Diamond K, who agreed to do the show for less than Frank Ski's asking price. "This is my first record, and I am, y'know, not in the place that I am now financially, let's say that," Diamond K says. "I wouldn't turn down nothin'! I didn't have a car, I was at my parents' house."

Diamond K's plan to make a little show money behind Frank Ski's back backfired when the concert was advertised on V103, during the station's top-rated show... which Frank Ski hosted. "Yeah, so, the first time I ever got cussed out was by Frank Ski," Diamond K says sheepishly. "And he told me about some other opportunities that were on the table, something that was comin' up with Luke, but I couldn't be trusted because I did this over a couple of thousand dollars."

To add insult to injury, the concert that Diamond K blew up his relationship with Frank Ski over wound up not even happening. "What was crazy about the whole situation is that it was during Christmastime, there was a snow storm, the show ended up being canceled anyway," Diamond K says with a laugh.

"He gave me the 'You'll never work in this town again' speech, right. And he's given that to other people, and they just, y'know, faded off the map never to be heard from again. But I was different than that, and so it motivated me," Diamond K says. "It was the best thing for me and I'm so glad that it happened that way. If we'd gone on and signed a bigger deal that I was involved in with Luke or somebody else, I would've screwed it all up at that time. So it worked out the way it was supposed to."

In 1996, the name 2 Hyped Brothers & A Dog returned for a second album, *The Doo Doo Project*, that featured several of the singles Frank Ski had released under his own name. It also included some of the most popular Miss Tony tracks, including "Pull Ya Gunz Out," and multiple sequels to "Whores in This House" ("Girls in The House," "Frats in The House"). The same year, Frank Ski left V103 to work at a competing station, Radio One's 92.3 (WERQ). And in 1998 he moved to Georgia, becoming an Atlanta radio institution for the next 20 years, and Frank Ski subsequently ceased releasing his own music or operating Deco Records.

Chapter 9
The Doo Dew Kidz

In the early days, producers and vocalists would collaborate on Baltimore club tracks, but few artists were both making beats and performing vocals. "Tapp and Tony and me, we was like *the* vocalists," Jimmy Jones told me in 2008, placing himself in a trinity of early Baltimore club voices alongside Miss Tony and Tapp, the rapper best known for 1994's "Shake That Ass." There were a few others who made several vocal cameos, like Unruly radio and retail promotions manager Antonio "Mr. Motts" Mottz, who appeared on DJ Kool Breez's 1997 track "Settle Outta Court" and, later on in the 2000s, K.W. Griff's "And I Say to Myself" and King Tutt's "Back of the Ac."

Jimmy Jones was sometimes credited as the sole artist and producer on tracks, but pretty much everything he made was in collaboration with DJ Boom or K.W. Griff – often all three of them worked together, whether or not under their collective name, Doo Dew Kidz. Booman and Griff credit Jones's taste and suggestions with frequently shaping their tracks, but Jones would downplay his involvement in the production as providing minor tweaks to their work. "I did some things as far as the tracks, just add a snare here, a beat there," Jones told me at his Glen Oaks home in 2008.

Jones wasn't an MC in hip hop terms but in the sense of the title's oldest definition, hosting parties at clubs like Odell's, Paradox, and Indigo. "He was one of the main masters of ceremonies, the guy on the mic doing shout-outs and hyping up the crowd," Booman told the *Baltimore Sun* in 2021. Even without the melodic range of a professional singer or the intricate rhymes of a rapper, Jones's personality and distinctive vocal tone cut through records that made him an ideal dance music vocalist, both on record and in the club.

Patrick "DJ Patrick" McDonald, born in 1971, was one of the first producers on the scene, along with DJ Class, who did regularly perform vocals on his own records. "More and more I got familiar with production, I started to venture out to more sounds, I was putting my own vocals [on the tracks]," he says. He made his debut with the *Quiet Records Presents DJ Patrick* EP, led by the track "Step to the Side," in 1993.

Quiet Records would release music by Griff and Booman, as well as Dukeyman, DJ Boobie, and many more, taking its place in the first wave of Baltimore club labels: Inner City, Unruly, Deco, Pimphouse, Baltimore Breakbeat Records, and Ear For Music. DJ Patrick's contributions to club music are often acknowledged by his peers, but he has rarely received the same kind of public recognition that others have, making the name Quiet Records something of an unfortunate self-fulfilling prophecy. "Man, crazy catalog," Booman says when Patrick's name comes up.

"I don't gripe over it, I just let my work show for itself," says DJ Patrick, who named one of his later mix CDs *Baltimore's Most Hated DJ*.

The competition between labels was largely friendly, though, and most of the labels were run by DJs who played each other's music. "We always made it that we could play whatever was hot," Scottie B. says. "That was one thing we made sure of, because Patrick had a bunch of hot shit, because Diamond had a bunch of hot shit, because Kenny got a bunch of hot shit, so it made it better. Everybody had a sound. You didn't wanna wear your sound out, so you played everybody."

In the early years of Unruly, a large share of the label's hot shit was coming from the Doo Dew Kidz. By the time Unruly was up and running, Griff and Booman had been making tracks for years, refining their craft and getting their music played in clubs, first Fantasy and then the Paradox, well before any of their music was pressed to vinyl. "We had tracks that were done and made, before we even knew that stuff was going on records," Booman says.

"We were just makin' 'em, puttin' 'em on cassette tapes and playin' 'em at parties and givin' 'em to DJs," Griff says. "Rod Braxton was one of the key players in spreading our music. Shawn Caesar had a residency every Friday at Fantasy's, Shawn would play from maybe midnight to 'bout 3pm, 3:30. Then Rod Braxton would play from 4 til the end of the night."

Back then, DJs would keep playing all the way until 7am. "You would come out of Fantasy, it'd be bright daylight," Booman laughs. "Going home like vampires. Crazy."

"Everybody would be looking for breakfast, didn't even wanna go home yet," Griff adds.

Griff and Booman's first sampler was the Gemini DS-1224. The first person in their circle of friends with a 4-track mixer was Elmer Mooring Jr. (later known as house music luminary DJ Scoob), who let Booman and Griff experiment with assembling songs. "We would take the sampler and make the loop and record it on the one track, and then go to the next track and started layerin' stuff, we started learning how to do that," Booman says. "We were tryin' to figure out how to make songs and make records."

One of Griff's first 4-track experiments was called "Pick It Up," which got played at the Paradox but never wound up on a record. Despite the similar titles, "Pick It Up" was unrelated to a later track, "Pick 'Em Up," that would eventually become one of the Doo Dew Kidz' signature records.

Griff and Booman upgraded to Ensoniq's EPS sampling keyboard when it hit the market in the late '80s, and then to Ensoniq's ASR-10 workstation in the early '90s. The latter wound up being the standard tool of the trade for most of Baltimore club's first generation of producers. "Everyone was using it," DJ Technics told Red Bull Music Academy in 2014. "It did nothing but sample and sequence. Load all your sounds in and you could make a song do anything. When we were using the ASR-10 it was the beginning of the digital era."

"That was the baby right there," Griff says, motioning to the ASR-10 in Booman's apartment and recalling the skilled producer who taught them how to use it, Ronnie Don. "He was the master of that ASR, he kinda walked us through that."

"That boy was everything," Booman nods in agreement.

After Booman mastered the ASR-10, he shared his knowledge with others. One of the budding East Baltimore producers he taught to work the machine was Rod Lee, born in 1973. "That's who turned me on to the ASR, Booman," says Lee. "I just went and bought everything I saw them have, but I bought the newer [model]. So the ASR-10, everybody had one with the red letters on it, I went and bought the blue one, so they're like, 'Oh, you on some big willie shit.'"

DJ Kool Breez entered the orbit of the Doo Dew Kidz around the same time. "I met Booman in like '92, '93. We used to go down to DJ's Outlet and hang out with Shawn and just bullshit all day, wasn't nothin' to do, just go there and hang out. That's where I met Booman at, me and him just kinda hit it off, both being really deep into record shit, that's what me and him really bonded over," Kool Breez remembers.

The Booman-produced Jimmy Jones track that made him a star and helped put Unruly on the map, "Watch Out for the Big Girl," dates back to around 1990, three years before it was ultimately released. "My cousin, I guess he had some kinda label or somethin'," Booman remembers. "He was like, 'Yeah, come down to the studio,' so I remember bringing the ASR down there and putting 'Big Girl' on a 2" tape. But nothing ever happened, he never tried to put it out or nothing like that, and then later on, y'know, it ended up at Unruly."

"'Watch Out for the Big Girl' was a song that Rod Braxton would play every once in a while, I didn't even know about it," Scottie B. remembers.

"But Jay Claxton said to me, 'It's this song that Rod plays every once in a while, he don't play a lot,' and he said how it went. So I never even heard this song. I called Jimmy, I said 'I need that song,' because I could hear it was gonna be something, it just wasn't getting pushed."

"Watch Out for the Big Girl" was originally inspired by a woman that was part of Miss Tony's entourage that the Doo Dew Kidz regularly encountered in the clubs (Miss Tony later recorded a similarly themed but unrelated song called "Big Girls" with singer Lucki and producer DJ Finesse). An early draft of "Watch Out" included more lyrics, including the word "bitch," which Booman vetoed, in favor dozens of different chopped-up variations of the same six words, "Watch out for the big girl."

The simplicity and ambiguity of the final version ultimately allowed big girls to embrace the song. In the fashion industry and in the trendy dance clubs of New York and Paris, the 1990s were the "waif era," a cultural moment when rail-thin supermodels were deemed the most attractive and stylish women. In Baltimore clubs, however, bodies of all sizes and shapes were welcome, and Doo Dew Kidz created an enduring anthem for larger women. Frank Ski put his own spin on the theme with the 2 Hyped Brothers track "Yo Big Girl It's Your World" in 1996.

DJ Booman eventually became Unruly's main studio engineer, although, he admits, "We didn't really know anything about engineering." Their work in the studio was largely intuitive, with lessons passed down from other DJs, not any college courses on recording. Griff was the one who had a special gift for taking all the different sections that had been constructed for a track and arranging them in a particular order to put the master recording down on an ADAT (Alesis digital audio tape). "We'd call him 'the mixdown,' because I hated sequencing records back then. So we would make stuff, and then give [it] to him to sequence, because he was better at sequencing records, like, hands down," says Booman.

"We would go somewhere like Scottie's house, and we would plug this up, put our disc in there. He would have the ADATs running, he would hit record, and say, 'Go,'" Griff adds.

"Just being able to see your name on a record, having your track on a record was really the high for me, I loved seeing that," Griff says.

"It was just so much fun just thinking of ideas and working on that thing. We never slept. Keep in mind, during this time, there weren't no kids, we weren't married, living at home, you're in your room, making tracks. Or I'd be on the phone with [Booman], I'd say, 'Listen to this, what do you think about this? It might need something. I'll come over tomorrow, you can listen to it and tell me what you think.' And that's pretty much what it was every day. Just this, record stores, this, eat food, school, back to this again."

Griff and Booman made plenty of tracks that were instrumentals or featured sampled vocals, but Jimmy Jones's voice remained a signature, and he rarely worked with other producers. Jones chanted the hooks of perennial club staples like "Set It Up Shorty" and "Where Y'All At" with a forceful yet gregarious bark, and even recorded perhaps Baltimore club's first Christmas song, "Doo Dew Xmas," in December 1996.

In 1996, the Doo Dew Kidz sampled New York girl group SWV's single "You're the One," a #1 hit on the R&B charts. The contagious club track "What's My Chance?" was released on the B-side of the Hardhead single "Wanna See Me?", and Booman and Griff's flip of the SWV track proved more popular than the original on Baltimore radio. SWV's label, RCA, saw this as a threat rather than an opportunity, serving Doo Dew Kidz with a cease-and-desist letter instead of buying the track and capitalizing on a regionally popular remix of the group's song.

It was an early instance of major labels failing to understand Baltimore club music's commercial potential – and perhaps a growing disconnect between Baltimore and the rest of the country, where house music and R&B had been headed in separate directions since the early '90s. It also served as a stern warning of the shaky legal ground the entire Baltimore club scene rested on: almost every song in the genre was created with uncleared samples, and if it ever got too big, it would attract a lot of attention from labels and copyright lawyers who'd see an opportunity to make some money in court.

For years, seeing their names on a record and hearing their own music in the Paradox was the thrill that kept Booman and Griff creating, what made them two of the most prolific producers in Baltimore, even though they weren't raking in huge sums of money. "It was exciting to hear, when you heard the tracks in the club and see the reaction was crazy, or to hear it on the radio. Like, it's musicians their whole life who can't say that," Booman says.

In fact, the Paradox's system, more than any studio monitors, was what the Doo Dew Kidz and many of their contemporaries used to determine if a track was complete. "The Paradox was our sound tester," Griff says. "We made tracks and stuff at either his place or mine or whatever. But once we were finished with it, we really didn't know how it was really gonna truly sound."

"We would tune our records to the club," Booman adds. "All they had was a Mackie 32.8 board and an ADAT machine, and we didn't really do a lot of compression and all that stuff. We just pushed the faders up to what we felt like it would sound good. If it sounded good in the Dox, that's how we pressed it."

Prince was famous for mixing his records slightly "in the red," pushing the volume into the danger zone where sounds got so loud that they started to distort. Booman and Griff operated the same way, much to the chagrin of A&R Record Manufacturing, the Florida factory that pressed their vinyl. "The pressing plants would call us back and tell us that the bass was too loud, and we were like, 'Nah, leave it the way it is.'"

Pressing plants customarily send clients test pressings to make sure the record sounds right before they mass produce hundreds or thousands of copies. "They give you five, and you give those to DJs, if you were smart, to try to get a buzz for the record before the full shipment comes back," says Diamond K.

Baltimore club producers would also purchase additional acetates from the manufacturer if they wanted to really go heavy on advance promotion for a single. "We would send off some DATs to Stan at A&R, and he would send us back acetates we could play in the meantime before the actual records came out," Griff says. "I still have all my acetates."

At one point, Griff and Booman learned the hard way that making records in a more conventional and technologically advanced environment didn't necessarily mesh with their sound. In 1997, Baltimore's perennially underfunded music scene received an influx of cash from an unlikely source: NFL wide receiver Michael Dwayne Jackson Dyson, better known as simply Michael Jackson. Jackson, who'd grown up in Louisiana, was traded from the Cleveland Browns to the Baltimore Ravens in 1996, and a year later he launched a record label in Baltimore called Big Play Entertainment, and opened a 53,000-square-foot recording studio on Biddle Street. "Wherever I am, I feel it is my home, and it's my job to give back to it," Jackson told the *Baltimore Sun* in 1997.

Big Play Entertainment signed Shai, the Washington, D.C., vocal group that topped the R&B charts in 1992 with "If I Ever Fall in Love," and Jackson poured money into an unsuccessful attempt to return the group to mainstream radio. But Big Play also made a significant investment into the homegrown sound of Baltimore club music, releasing EPs by Dukeyman, DJ Class, and DJ Technics. Big Play teamed with Unruly Records for the *Unruly Club Classics Volume 1* compilation, perhaps the earliest attempt to canonize Baltimore club's definitive songs – its selections included "Watch Out for the Big Girl," DJ Class's "Roldatshit," DJ Technics' "Push It to the Ceiling," Karizma's "Blow (Scottie B. Remix)," and Dukeyman's "Shorty You Phat."

DJ Booman and K.W. Griff's 1998 album for Big Play, *When We Were Little*, was one of the few proper full-length albums any Baltimore club act made in the '90s, when singles and EPs were the preferred formats of the genre. Unfortunately, Big Play tried to clean up the Doo Dew Kidz sound, and the results didn't sound right, despite good material. "They had all of these big-time engineers, and they compressed the shit out of the record, and it drained the life out of every track on there. So those tracks never got played, to this day," says Booman. "If you play 'em off the vinyl, there's no life in 'em at all, they're just flat."

Baltimore club artists keeping their 12" releases short was partly a strategic move to get out more releases, but also to maximize the sound of the music. The longer a vinyl record is, the quieter the music on it is, with more audible noise when you turn up the volume. Even the three full-length songs on each side of *When We Were Little* proved to be suboptimal for music made to reverberate through the Paradox. "We always try to do two per side, three is pushin' it. Maybe one or two of those releases may have had four, but that's because it had a little a cappella at the end," Griff says. "We wanted to make sure that any of those records that we put out were nice and loud. You didn't have to turn everything up."

The studio on Biddle Street remained open for a few years, and DJ Class also recorded there. But the Big Play experiment was ultimately short-lived, and the Baltimore club music released on the label didn't make the same impact as the producers' releases on their own imprints. Michael Dwayne Jackson Dyson left Baltimore in 1999 to briefly play for the Seattle Seahawks before retiring from the NFL. Jackson was elected mayor of Tangipahoa, Louisiana, in 2009, and died in a 2017 motorcycle accident at the age of 48.

By the end of the '80s, compact discs had overtaken vinyl as the top selling physical format for music. And while classic album reissues, or a big-name act releasing an album on vinyl before it was available on CD would cause an occasional spike in vinyl sales, it was truly DJs who kept vinyl alive in the '90s. Baltimore club was only a small part of the global dance music community and the hip hop nation that ensured that labels kept releasing music on vinyl, but it was an active part of the DJ community.

In the 2010s and 2020s, vinyl sales have surged as a new generation have come to embrace the 12" record, and pop artists like Taylor Swift and Adele have broken records for vinyl sales. It's unlikely, however, that vinyl pressing plants would have even survived long enough to enjoy this resurgence if not for '90s DJs (and some plants didn't survive – A&R Record Manufacturing closed down in 2015).

The rise of Serato, an Australian software company whose products allowed DJs to scratch and beatmatch on a virtual turntable without actual records, was what finally led some DJs to move away from vinyl in the new millennium. CDDJ, a product that allows you to DJ with compact discs and "scratch" with them like vinyl, also changed the game to a lesser extent.

Emmanual "DJ Manny" Wheele, born in 1985, was part of a generation that learned to DJ the old-fashioned way with vinyl, but was an early adopter of CDDJ. "They just kinda criticized me on usin' CDs, but I'm still mixin' live like everybody else," DJ Manny says. "Everybody was so scared and skeptical of usin' Serato. They turn around and now everybody's got Serato."

Many of Baltimore's older DJs like K.W. Griff eventually made the switch to Serato, making it easy to play the classics alongside newer club music that may only be available on CD or MP3. In fact, in 2007 Scottie B. sold his entire vinyl collection to the Baltimore record store True Vine, and DJ Technics put a large amount of vinyl up for sale around the same time.

Chapter 10
Are You the Bomb?

"I don't know, I just thought I'd move to Baltimore and start a label," Stephen Janis recalls. It was 1992, and Janis, a White journalist and New York native, was working as a fact checker for magazines like *Rolling Stone* and *Esquire*. "I had a friend who was living here, and I just thought y'know, well, it's a different kind of city, I couldn't really afford to live in New York. And I thought maybe I'd move to a place that was cheaper, there was sort of an interesting scene."

Janis's label, CLR, was based on Aliceanna Street in Fells Point, and he sighs deeply when I ask him what those letters stood for. "My partner was a weird dude, and he wanted to call it Chicken Lips Records. I was like, 'I don't wanna do that.' I know, it's so dumb." Janis was interested in documenting the local hip hop scenes in Baltimore and Washington, D.C., as well as regional styles like go-go. CLR's biggest success story was DJ Kool from Washington, D.C., whose 1996 single "Let Me Clear My Throat" became a massive mainstream hit.

Baltimore's regional sound, club music, was still in its relative infancy. And Janis didn't necessarily recognize it as its own genre, distinct from hip hop, when CLR released singles like Foe's "Stretch Marks" and Tapp's "Buck Move," which essentially featured rapping over Baltimore club beats. "At that point, I don't know if I knew it was Baltimore club, I just knew it was, like, a Baltimore record," Janis says. "We were just doing like any independent label, picking up people who were in the community who were doing stuff."

Eventually, CLR did recognize that this Baltimore sound, whatever it was called, had a strong following not just in Baltimore stores but nationally and even internationally. "We sold a lot at Music Liberated," he says. "We took a lot of export [orders] too. A big market for us was this distributor called Unique Distribution. And the club stuff, what was Baltimore club, would do really well for some reason. They would order like two or thee thousand copies at a time, which doesn't sound like a lot, but for a little independent label that was actually quite amazing." Hanging out at Music Liberated, Janis began to meet Baltimore club producers that he'd go on to work with like Rod Lee and DJ Class.

After Diamond K's brief taste of stardom as a rapper, and his abrupt dismissal from Deco Records by Frank Ski, he decided to start over from scratch (no pun intended), as a DJ. He took a job at Electronics & More in Westview Mall, working alongside DJ Kenny B. "It was good, because I started to see what DJs would come into the store to buy, and what they wanted, and what they were looking for. And slowly I started to understand how to move, what type of records do what, and I became very involved in the DJ culture," Diamond K says.

"I would go to parties with Kenny and carry his records in, carry his speakers in, set up. And then he would let me mix early. I mixed in the store when I got off work, and I'm off work, off the clock, but I would still be there mixing, practicing. And that's how I started to build my name as a DJ. And then I just made what I consider the natural progression to producing." Diamond K had produced his own original demo for "Where's Ya Boyfriend At" before it was re-recorded with Frank Ski, but now he was taking beatmaking more seriously. "I feel the best producers are also DJs, because they have a certain ear, and they can understand the flow, what is required, what vocals go with what tracks."

Diamond K founded Pimphouse Records in 1995, even though he had friends at the club music labels that already existed, including Scottie B. "Our relationship goes back to before there was an Unruly. And at the onset of Unruly, when they were planning it out, he told me he wanted me to get involved. But I didn't," Diamond K says, citing his ambitious nature and his desire to control his own destiny after bristling under Frank Ski's leadership. "I'm different. And so I knew that it wasn't gonna work if I was there, because I'm gonna do what I wanna do."

Like DJ Equalizer, Diamond K started out making a series of breakbeat records for other DJs, *Diamond K's Big Ass Breaks*, before releasing proper songs of his own. "[Equalizer] was definitely a mentor of mine, and somebody who was really helpful for me," Diamond K says, quickly adding under his breath, "even though he's a Trump supporter."

Rather than following up "Where's Ya Boyfriend At" and continuing to release music as a rapper, Diamond K was interested in producing club tracks for other vocalists. "I didn't even think of doing my own stuff, I felt like working with some artists," he says. In 1995, he ran into CLR rapper Foe, and proposed working together on a remix of "Stretch Marks." "He said he wanted to do something new, instead of remixing that song, which I liked even better."

Foe and Diamond K's first collaboration, "Are You the Bomb?", was a potent fusion of hip hop and Baltimore club, with male and female call-and-response vocals. The female counterpoint vocal came from a girl Foe brought to the studio, credited as "Spanish Fly" on the original release and later sometimes as "Spanish Fli." "He dated a Spanish girl, and she was in the studio with us, and she had some girls with her. So they were kinda singin' some stuff in the studio and we ended up incorporating that as a breakdown," Diamond K says. "I have a very simple formula for records. The hook is super important to me, and the breakdown. I'm always gonna have a breakdown in the middle or some kind of bridge at the end."

The song was engineered by Jay Funk at Tic Toc Studios in the same year that he produced some of Baltimore's most revered hip hop of the '90s with the group the Annexx Click, whose rugged boom-bap sound had no trace of club music. Diamond K programmed a distinctive, hard-hitting drum pattern for "Are You the Bomb?" on an EPS-16+, with a shimmying "Sing Sing" loop layered over it as a hi-hat.

In the years since "Doo Doo Brown," Baltimore club had moved towards simpler, more repetitive tracks that might contain only one or two lines of repeated lyrics, and "Are You the Bomb?" went against the grain. "I thought the record was different than anything that was being played at that time, his vocals were different, and y'know, it was definitely not what was happening at that time," says Diamond K. For the 12" release, Diamond K paired "Are You the Bomb?" with a more conventional club track called "Don't Front (Give It Up)," credited to the C.I.A. (Cash In Abundance), that riffed on "Face Down, Ass Up" by 2 Live Crew and sampled Boyz II Men. "It was more in line with what was going on, it was just a hook with a sample, and that was it. It wasn't any rap with it, it was really simple."

Diamond K knew "Are You the Bomb?" had more potential, but that "Don't Front" was an easier sell to Baltimore DJs. So he used some clever misdirection to bring more attention to the other side of the record while distributing test pressings of the single to DJs. "They gravitated to the other record first, which is what I expected," he says. "It's a white label record, so you gotta handwrite what the song is on the record. And so what I had my assistant do was purposefully mislabel it, hoping that a DJ might mistakenly play the song that we really were pushing, which was 'Are You The Bomb?'"

"And that did happen, and Reggie Reg played it because it's mistakenly labeled. He was thinking he was playing the other song. He played it on the air on V103, this was the summer of '95, and it instantly got a great reaction, and we kind of took off with it from there," Diamond K says. The real vindication of the success of "Are You the Bomb?" is that he won back the respect of the man who'd fired him. "Later on that summer, Frank Ski called me and, y'know, said that he was wrong, and he helped me a lot after that."

Diamond K patterned himself after Frank Ski, with more conventional promotional strategies like music videos and regional live performances with onstage vocalists, while most other Baltimore club labels were primarily concerned with making records DJs in the city would play. "I always wanted vocals attached to it, so you can perform a song, that was always my thing. A lot of my contemporaries just wanted to sample hooks of rappers or stuff, and y'know, I wanted to be an artist, and I patterned it after artists that were mainstream, y'know. So you have a music video, you have posters, and these type of things."

He hired "Doo Doo Brown" director Chris Robinson to make an "Are You the Bomb?" video, and did shows with

Foe up and down the East Coast. "We did Philly, we did Richmond, we did Jersey, D.C., and of course Baltimore. And so the record's going, I'm strategically working the record with DJs in each one of those markets, and we're building the record," Diamond K says. "We had a good set. I would come out first, talk to the crowd, and I would perform one of my songs, from the turntables, bring him out, and then we would do 'Stretch Marks' and 'Are You the Bomb?'"

Kenny B and DJ Boobie made Diamond K's music a staple at Hammerjacks, much as Rod Braxton had done for the Doo Dew Kidz at Paradox. "I had the connections at Hammerjacks and V103. And so we're just breaking records, so we're talking about thousands of people every Sunday and Friday in Hammerjacks, and Louie Louie's on Fridays. I was doing mixtapes at the flea market, the music is spreading."

One person who was a little jealous that "Are You the Bomb?" wasn't his song was Miss Tony. "After I started my label, I wanted him to let me produce some songs for him, and he was telling me, 'Okay, I'm gonna do that,'" Diamond K remembers. "I would've more than likely given the track of 'Are You the Bomb?' to Tony, but it just so happened that me and Foe connected, y'know, and it just worked out like that. And so Tony was like, 'You gave him that track, that was supposed to be me.' And so he's quote-unquote 'mad at me' for this, right, so then he didn't wanna do a track."

There's a popular remix of "Are You the Bomb?" that is sometimes erroneously credited to Miss Tony that was actually Foe doing a hilariously convincing impression.

"Tony's not fuckin' with me, so he's not trying to do it. So Foe says, 'I can sound like Tony,' so we have a remix where he's like, 'See me is to love me, ride me like a pony.' Foe does that imitating Tony. But it was funny because everybody thought that it was Tony."

That remix came about largely by accident during the session for the original song. "We're in the studio, sometimes things go wrong, they say, 'Hey, wait a minute, let's take a second,'" Foe told 92Q host AJ Showtime in an interview on the station's program *Rap Attack* in October 2024.

> "So when that happened, I started singing 'See me is to love me.' I did not know that Diamond K recorded it. So later on, when he was about to put the record out, him and [Supa DJ Big L] actually begged me to let them put it out, because I was like, 'No. I don't even sound right!' But L kept pushin' and pushin' and pushin', and that was that."

Eventually, when they were back on good terms, Diamond K and Miss Tony recorded and performed together again. And Tony was a good enough sport about people believing he was on the "Are You the Bomb?" remix that he would perform the track. "Because, he said, 'he imitating me, then…' and everybody thought it was him anyway," Diamond K says.

"'Are You the Bomb?' was an amazing run," Diamond K says. Unfortunately, things soured between him and Foe before they could fully capitalize on the song or make more music together.

> "We didn't have a recording contract done. And so as we're picking up airplay in different states and the record is on the verge of taking off, I'm getting calls from larger labels. The other thing is, it was awkward because he's older than me, but I'm the director of this whole thing, and he's not agreeing with some of my ideas."

By the time they made the video, "We were communicating through attorneys."

"Are You the Bomb?" remains well remembered in Baltimore, but Diamond K still wonders what it could've done if he hadn't pulled the plug on continuing promotion of the song, and thinks of it as a music industry cautionary tale. "The worst thing that can happen is you can have a hit record before you're ready for a hit record. That's, to me, even worse than having no hit record, because it's like a water hose, and you're trying to grab it and it's just going everywhere."

Fortunately, Diamond K's friction with Foe led to an even more legendary track. It started when a friend from the club scene, DJ Mickey, brought a vocalist to Diamond K's attention. "He'd come to me with an idea with an artist, and I think he dated her sister. But he came to me with this girl who's Big Ria, she's a young, young girl," he remembers. "I would say that she was 20, she might have been 21, but she sounded younger than she was."

"It was well known at this time that Foe and I were feuding," Diamond K says. "So [DJ Mickey] had a concept where she was dissing Foe on the 'Are You the Bomb?' beat. And I loved it. I said, 'We're putting this out.'" He returned to Tic Toc Studios with DJ Mickey and Big Ria to put together the song.

Answer records have a long history in popular music, and took on a greater potency in the hip hop era. The success of the Brooklyn rap group UTFO's 1984 hit "Roxanne, Roxanne" prompted dozens of answer records, many of them from young women claiming to be the subject of the song. The most famous of them, Queens rapper Roxanne Shante, launched her career with "Roxanne's Revenge."

"The Answer (Am I a Bomb?)" was supposed to be Big Ria's star-making moment as she roasted the male voice on the song, a stand-in for Foe. She didn't actually have beef with Foe, but she was an entertaining mouthpiece for Diamond K to air his grievances with a former collaborator. When it was released, it didn't make much of an impact. "Evidently, the only person that was mad at [Foe] was me," Diamond K shrugs. Fortunately, they'd made a B-side for the song that proved to be the real hit.

"I said 'We need another song,'" Diamond K says.

"After I sat on it and thought about it, I said that this is a reaction record, this is not an original record. An answer record's only gonna have the life of the original, and once the original's over, that record is, y'know, not as relevant. And so that's why 'Hey U Knuckleheads' came in."

Part of the hyper local appeal of Baltimore club music was that vocalists and DJs would frequently shout out familiar people, places, and things in the city. Baltimore had a relatively small place in pop culture, especially in the 1990s, but these songs that played on the radio and in packed clubs let a downtrodden city celebrate itself in a way that TV shows, films, and pop music rarely did. "People looked at club music as theirs," Scottie B. told *True Laurels* in 2014. "A lot of the shouting out neighborhoods and if you mentioned someone in a song, it was a good chance that your listener knew who that was. There was a lot of ground support."

In that context, it's easy to understand why "Knuckleheads" became a Baltimore club classic – it's the ultimate shoutout record. "'Hey U Knuckleheads' took off instantly. That was a fun ride there," Diamond K says. The track is less than two minutes long, but the first verse is a compact geography lesson about Black Baltimore, as Big Ria rattles off the names of 43 places in 45 seconds, including street names (such as Whitelock), specific intersections (Edmondson and Pulaski), neighborhoods (Cherry Hill), housing projects (Murphy Homes), and even a suburb in Baltimore County (Catonsville).

"And then I had to add my street, which is a very small street called Bernice Street," Diamond K says. "And of course, nothing happens on Bernice Street" (the name of the street he lived on is actually Bernice Avenue, but it's hard to argue with Diamond K after he immortalized it on record as Bernice Street).

Not everybody loved the Baltimore geography lesson in "Hey U Knuckleheads," though. "I got a lot of flak for that song at the time," Diamond K says. "People in the street were saying, like, 'You're making our spot hot,' and 'You're telling the police where to go.' That kinda thing."

Part of what made the song pop was Big Ria's voice. She sounded even younger than she was, almost like a kid, and her Baltimore accent was as thick as any ever heard on record. The Baltimore accent, as linguist Kara Becker explained to *Baltimore Fishbowl* in 2014, is characterized by "fronting back vowels." Those are sounds that Baltimoreans pronounce with their tongue in the front of their mouth, when speakers from other regions would usually keep their tongue in the back of their mouth. It's especially noticeable in long O sounds, turning a word like "loose" into "lewse." And when Big Ria says "Hey you knuckleheads, walkin' down the avenue," the way she draws out "you" and the last syllable of "avenue" is a pure, perfectly distilled example of a Baltimore accent.

Big Ria was just Ria when she first came to Tic Toc Studios, but Diamond K had designs on patterning her image after a New York rapper who'd broken out as a major star in the mid-'90s. "I hate to say this, but my vision of her was always Lil Kim. I wanted her to be Lil Kim. She didn't wanna be that.

So we have this back and forth, and of course, I wanted her to be Lil Ria, but she didn't wanna be that, she wanted to be Big Ria, so that's what we did," he says. The counterintuitive name may have still helped her become a star, though. "People love Ria. She's short, little. She's called Big Ria but she's not big at all."

"Hey U Knuckleheads" and "The Answer" weren't really the kind of songs that were built to launch an artist as a sex symbol, but Diamond K marketed her that way. The 12" was packaged with a provocative publicity photo of Big Ria in a revealing dress, holding her breasts. The vinyl label referred to the A-side as "left nipple" and the B-side as "right nipple."

Ultimately, Diamond K and Big Ria had completely different ideas about how she should be presented to the public, and one night that conflict came to a head. "I remember one show, I promoted her a certain way, I wanted her to be sexy and we did her posters and flyers like that. And I sent my assistant with her to go get an outfit for the show, gave her the money, 'Go get her what she wants,'" he remembers. "We get to the show, she has like this big bulky sweatsuit on, and I'm like, 'Hey, hurry up and go change.' And [my assistant]'s like, 'No, this is what she has.'"

Performing in sweats instead of the kind of low-cut dress she wore in promotional photos, Big Ria faced a hostile audience. "We bring her on the stage, and they instantly are booing, like, 'Who is this? What is this?'"

"The Answer (Am I a Bomb?)" was dropped from Big Ria's live shows after Diamond K reconciled with Foe, who had no hard feelings about Ria recording the diss track about him. "He knew that I was the [songwriter] and she had no problem with him," Diamond K says. "So sometimes I would have Foe and Ria perform together."

In 1996, Diamond K had reconnected with the first friend he'd made in the local music scene, Dukeyman, and they became close collaborators. "He comes in the record store and, y'know, just catchin' up, he's working on some songs, and he's playin' me some records, and we end up goin' in the studio."

Aside from his work at Tic Toc Studios, Diamond K was frequently making his records in DIY home studios, like many of his peers. "I'll use the word 'studio' a lot of times but this was the attic, his bedroom at his mother's house in Milford Mill. And so, if it had studio equipment in any room, I call it the studio," Diamond K says. "After that we probably did, I don't know, 50 songs together. We were really really really good friends."

Diamond K's first collaboration with Dukeyman, which he released under the label name C.I.A. Records instead of Pimphouse, was "Werkitt '96 Style," which sampled a couple of tracks that had been house music staples for several years. One was the British duo DNA's hit 1990 remix of Suzanne Vega's "Tom's Diner." The other was "Work This Pussy," a 1989 track Junior Vasquez released under the alias Boom-Boom that, in retrospect, resembles what Baltimore club would eventually sound like as closely as anything from the '80s.

Diamond K continued releasing songs, often with vocals by himself and a rotating cast of collaborators. "I saw that I wanted to build a label, with other artists, y'know, under my umbrella." "Put Ya Leg Up" in particular caught on in Philadelphia better than his other releases. "'Are You the Bomb?', they didn't get it, initially," he says. "'Put Ya Leg Up' was different there."

At the peak of Big Ria's popularity, Diamond K assembled

a new group, Da Horsemen, that were part of her live shows. "When Ria did a show at Hammerjacks, I took them on the stage with me to kinda hype the crowd up," he says. "They were like backup for her. And then I said, 'They need records,' and so we started doing songs. I wrote things for them to say, and they did those and then we started doing performances with them too."

Da Horsemen were named after the Four Horsemen, a popular team of professional wrestlers led by Ric Flair in the '80s and '90s. "The original guys were all wrestling fans, we watched wrestling before we went to the club, like it was based in wrestling," Diamond K says. "These were all guys that used to hang in the store with me, and they were in the club with me, and they would be dancin' in the club and I'm just like, 'This is a group.'"

One of the original members of Da Horsemen was one of Diamond K's oldest friends from West Baltimore Middle School. Johnny "Porkchop" Doswell, born in 1973, had the kind of raspy, distinctive voice and gift for rhyming that probably would've made him a more conventional rap star if he was from New York. But he was also game to perform the lyrics Diamond K wrote for Da Horsemen, and Porkchop would eventually become a major figure in club music. "He's a much better rapper than I am, stylistically," says Diamond K.

At the time, New York still dominated the mainstream hip hop landscape. And while Maryland is below the Mason-Dixon line, and there are many ways in which it's a southern state, Baltimore hip hop was still largely following New York's lead in the '90s, both at the underground level and in terms of radio playlists. Diamond K recalls being one of the first DJs in the city, however, to embrace the rising tide of southern hip hop, particularly the New Orleans labels No Limit and Cash Money.

"I definitely was the first person here in Baltimore playing No Limit and Cash Money records in the club," he says. "Here, it was heavy New York, you know, Wu-Tang, Jay-Z. Whatever was the New York style, which was all good with me too, but I'm the person that's like, 'Okay, but we also have this.'"

Da Horsemen's early singles "We Boys" and "We Bout It" bear the clear influence of No Limit, particularly the latter, which echoes TRU's hit "I'm Bout It, Bout It" and even features an "ughhh!" ad lib reminiscent of Master P. It was still very much Baltimore club music, though, with chants and shout outs instead of rhyming couplets. "Not necessarily 16-bar verses," says Diamond K. "Just sing-songy kind of things."

Despite the "four horsemen" theme, Da Horsemen grew into a much bigger social clique with more than four members. "As it got popular, we would dress alike," Diamond K says.

> "To me, if a group is not unified in their clothing, they're not a group, you're just a bunch of guys. And so what started happening is that other guys would try to emulate the group, and then each guy would start bringing a friend, and then next thing you know, it was a larger group of people."

Da Horsemen opened Baltimore concerts by mainstream acts including Missy Elliott and 112. In addition to Diamond K and Porkchop, several members of Da Horsemen went on to have long careers as DJs, producers, performers, or hosts in the Baltimore club and hip hop scenes, including DJ Say Wut, Supa DJ Big L, BJ Da Chozen 1ne, Wes Raven, Love Jones,

Cookieman, Frankie Baby, Ted Skola, Bean, Tug, DJ Unique, Devious, and Wacko.

After a few years, the first incarnation of Da Horsemen ran its course, as members disagreed on musical decision, and Diamond K's ambitions to make moves outside Baltimore with the group. "My goal, I think, was different from other people's goal, and that caused us to have a rift," Diamond K says. "My thing was, 'Let's get us out of the city,' and their thing was, 'We wanna do the city stuff.' And then Pork didn't agree with some of my direction, Say Wut didn't agree with some of my direction, and I said, 'Okay, go do it your way.'"

In the early 2000s, Diamond K renamed his label High Rolla Records. He began to feel self-conscious about the original name when he was invited back to Edmondson-Westside High School as a distinguished alumnus.

"They were honoring me and DJ Boobie, who also went to Edmondson. And they announced me as the CEO of Pimphouse Music, and they said it out loud, and there are kids there, and it hit me at that moment, 'I cannot be called that,'" he says. "It seemed cool in my head, and in the nightclubs. But in my high school and any other places where there were kids, it seemed super crazy. And so at that moment, I changed it to High Rolla Records. I can't do anything with the Pimphouse [tattoo] that's on my arm, but it's all good."

Chapter 11
Tear Da Club Up

Although Unruly Records had been releasing music for years at that point, Shawn Caesar and Scottie B. didn't officially incorporate the label as an LLC and set up an office space until the summer of 1996. "Shawn took it to the next level," says DJ Kool Breez, who had begun releasing music on Unruly and HardHead a year earlier, sometimes solo and sometimes with DJ Big Red under the group name 2 Whyte Kydz. "He was like, 'This could be structured a little better.' He wanted to get it now goin' as a business, and everybody had a position. We're all still down there to do music, but he was gonna start a payroll and everything."

Unruly's office was on 310 Park Avenue – it probably goes without saying that Park Avenue in midtown Baltimore is not quite as upscale as Park Avenue in New York City. Kool Breez was put in charge of the Unruly Record Pool. "It got so big so fast," Kool Breez says. "I remember we were getting serviced from I think 90 labels. We were doing pretty good, we got to the point where we had 75 members."

Unfortunately, hip hop labels were still merely looking at Baltimore as a market for promoting their existing artists, not as an untapped scene where they could recruit new talent. "It was cool because it got me in touch with a lot of people in the industry, but it didn't get me in touch with them on the terms that I wanted," Kool Breez says. "I wanted to get in touch with these motherfuckers like, 'Yeah, I got beats.'"

DJ Kool Breez had a distinctive sound on early releases like his "Shades of Red" single that came partly from him using different gear from most of his contemporaries. As a hip hop head who revered Gang Starr producer DJ Premier, Kool Breez took an interest in using the same equipment Premier used. So he worked with the SP-1200, a sampling drum machine produced by E-mu Systems, instead of the ASR-10, the keyboard-based workstation that had been Baltimore club's standard. "I knew how to the use the ASR and all, but I just always recorded on the SP."

Kool Breez considers 1997's *A Day in the Life of a Whyte Kid* EP to be an unheralded gem of his catalog. "I did some different shit on there," he says, singling out the song "Uh Uh," which used the same spacey mallet percussion from a 1973 record by jazz drummer Shelly Manne that DJ Premier had sampled on Jeru the Damaja's rap hit "Come Clean." "It's stuff on there that people don't even know what's goin' on, but I know it's there. If only y'all heard it the way I heard it."

For most of the '90s, Unruly did the lion's share of its business in 10 to 15 stores in the Baltimore area, and the remainder was primarily sold in Philadelphia – which remained Baltimore club's biggest secondary market for many years – or in Virginia. "We had a couple stores in Philly, Funk-o-Mart and Armand's, and we were goin' a lot through Liaison Records for distribution, so [other stores] would have to get it from them," Scottie B. says.

When Baltimore club first started building a fanbase in Philadelphia, however, the Baltimore labels were getting cut out of the profits. "Around '94 we started hearing they were bootlegging our shit in Philly," Scottie B. told *True Laurels* in 2014. "So we went up there and it was true. It was really hurting us in such a small market. We started getting cool with the record stores to find out who was doing it."

Washington, D.C., is much closer to Baltimore than Philadelphia is, but perhaps because D.C. already had a dominant local sound in go-go, club music spread a little more easily up to Philly. And while Chuck Brown was the undisputed founding father of go-go, Baltimore club was a more diffuse group effort – Frank Ski and others had credible claims to being the top DJ in Baltimore in particular eras, but nobody was ever permanently the "face" of the genre like Chuck Brown.

British art rock producer Brian Eno coined the term "scenius" to describe the collective intelligence and creativity that develops within a closely collaborative and competitive community of artists. Music critics love to anoint individual artists as geniuses, and also love to celebrate local music scenes where a whole assortment of exciting likeminded artists seem to spring up together. Eno suggested that the truth is usually a more nuanced combination of those two narratives. Many Baltimore club producers were individually brilliant and shaped the genre, but the scenius that they shared was more powerful than any one person's contribution.

The cross-pollination between Baltimore and Washington did happen eventually, partly because so many DJs worked in clubs or on the radio in both markets. "It surprises me sometimes, it's like two different worlds 30 miles apart," says James Nasty, a producer and DJ who grew up in a Maryland suburb of D.C. He was a big go-go fan who only knew a little of the Baltimore sound that was bubbling upstate until he attended the University of Maryland Baltimore County. "I didn't know too much about club music through high school, I knew a couple of the bigger songs like 'Doo Doo Brown,'

'Watch Out For The Big Girl.' I came up here for college and I first experienced club music, I was like…'I love this stuff too.'" Remaining in Baltimore after college, he became a prolific club music producer.

Throughout the '90s, as hip hop became big business, rappers from all over the country, including the Deep South and the West Coast, were selling millions. And while a wealth of mainstream hip hop came from New York, New Jersey, and Philadelphia, there was a conspicuous lack of national stars coming out of Baltimore and Washington, D.C., two majority-Black cities on the East Coast. At a certain point, go-go and Baltimore club became a scapegoat for the region's relative lack of success in hip hop, a perennial debate that continues to rage on.

The closest thing Baltimore had to a national rap hit in that decade was Sagat's 1994 single "Why Is It? (Funk Dat)," which fared better on the UK charts than in America. The song featured a house beat, and was released on the dance label Max Records, but wasn't really Baltimore club in any meaningful sense.

A few R&B acts from Baltimore, like the groups Dru Hill and Ruff Endz, did hit the big time in the '90s. Dru Hill member Sisqo released his debut solo *Unleash the Dragon* in 1999, featuring the lead single "Got to Get It" and the massive crossover hit "Thong Song." Def Jam released a 12" single for "Thong Song" in 2000 with several remixes, including "Got to Get It (B-More Club Mix)." The remix is a credible Baltimore club track that contains elements of "NaNaNa," a Mystikal-sampling club hit by DJ Technics and DJ Class. The 12" only credits the remix to the producers of the original "Got to Get It," Sisqo himself and Al West, but DJ Class confirmed in

2025 that he made the remix. It is probably the first instance of a Baltimore club track appearing on a major label release.

A couple of the most transformative rappers of the '90s had roots in Baltimore. Tupac Shakur spent some of his formative years in Baltimore, attending Roland Park Middle School and the Baltimore School for the Arts, before moving to California and becoming an icon of West Coast rap. DMX spoke many times of living in Baltimore before launching his career in Yonkers, New York. Both of them had forceful voices that made them ideal candidates to be sampled in Baltimore club tracks – and both were, many times. DJ Class's "Come Quick See" is the most popular 2Pac-sampling Baltimore club track. And DMX's voice has graced a number of club staples, including King Tutt's "That's How We Do It," DJ Ron Rico's "What You Heard," and Rod Lee's "Tear It Up."

In fact, the loudest and rowdiest sounds in hip hop almost always tended to make the best Baltimore club samples, like the vocal loop from New York rap group Onyx sampled on one of Griff and Booman's biggest hits, "Pick 'Em Up." And in the late '90s, when DMX's Ruff Ryders crew and their producer Swizz Beatz were blowing up, DJ Class sampled the blaring synth horn fanfare from the Swizz track for Drag-On and Juvenile's "Down Bottom."

The combination of Class's voice and the Swizz Beatz synths on "Tear Da Club Up" was explosive in Baltimore clubs in 1999. "Get your life" had become a signature Baltimore slang term for seizing the day and having a good time, and it got its biggest on-record use in Class's hook for the track ("If you came to get your life, tear the fuckin' club up").

DJ Class, who debuted as a hip hop artist with the 1992 single "Class Is in Session," didn't release Baltimore club tracks as often as some of his contemporaries. But he was always popular and respected in the club scene for the high quality and sonic variety of his output, including hits like "Roldatshit," "The Love Theme," and "Wuz Up Baby." "I have been known for taking a little break in between records," Class says. "I always joke and kid and say that I'm four different people wrapped in one."

"Class alone, he'd have one song that would play all year," Dukeyman told me in 2006. "And it hit like it just came out, every time you play it."

"DJ Class is, in my estimation, just an amazingly talented guy," says Stephen Janis.

"['Tear Da Club Up'] is just such an awesome encapsulation of the spirit of the city. And you could tell that was coming right from the club, but he was turning it into something that became an anthem. I just think he's a great songwriter. I watched him work in the studio, he could so quickly formulate a song."

Unruly had high hopes that "Tear Da Club Up" could work outside Baltimore, and went up to New York to promote the record at influential spots like the Brooklyn record store Beat Street. "We were like, 'If this one don't do it, this ain't gon' happen.' And we take it to Beat Street, to the DJ in there, and dropped 'em off, heard nothin'. We said, 'Fuck it. Okay, this ain't gonna happen outside here,'" Scottie B. says. "And then, y'know, almost ten years later, somebody gave us the heads-up that Funk Flex is playing [Baltimore club] on Hot 97."

In fact, Unruly made several attempts to break into the hip hop and dance music mainstream via trips to New York over the course of the '90s. Tierre Brownlee recalls accompanying Scottie B. to Uptown Records, when it was one of the hottest labels in the industry, to pitch Unruly's first hip hop release,

Sparrow's "Physics," to Virgil Simms, a Baltimore native who had become an Uptown exec. On another occasion, Caesar, Scottie B., and Brownlee paid a visit to one of the most famous DJs on the planet, Junior Vasquez, to try to get him to play an Unruly release. It was a much different, much more glamorous world than they were used to from Baltimore's nightspots. "I remember this like it was yesterday, Junior Vasquez had a pink couch in his DJ booth," Brownlee says.

Unruly may have struggled to get respect in New York, but they were the gold standard in Baltimore. "I was competitive with Unruly, Patrick's label, Rod Lee, anybody, because I think that the best Baltimore club music was made in the '90s, and it was the best because we were all competitive. Everybody wanted to be the best," Diamond K says.

> "And so I would hear a song that Unruly released, a Griff and Booman, and it was just like 'Oh, I gotta come with something better than that.' And I feel like they did the same thing. And that competition, that friendly competition really got some really good music recorded and released."

Today, though, Diamond K does wonder if things could have gone better if everybody was on the same page. "In hindsight, what should've happened is that all of us should've worked together, because everybody brought something to the table," he says. "If we all worked together to push our artists, to use our resources, the movement would have been nationwide. But, y'know, competition and ego never allowed for that to happen, sadly."

When I relayed Diamond K's sentiments to Scottie B., he agreed that Baltimore club probably would've gotten further with more coordination and teamwork. "Oh, a hundred times. A hundred times."

In the summer of 1999, Unruly and its promo arm, DOT Promotions ("doin' our thing"), began a business partnership with Downtown Locker Room (DTLR), a Baltimore retail chain founded in 1983 that specializes in streetwear. After Shawn Caesar met with DTLR co-founder Rick Levin, though, he disappeared for a few days, leaving the label's staff in the dark about the changes that were afoot. "Shawn kinda dropped everything and ran to Downtown Locker Room. We thought he just didn't show up for work one day and none of us could find him," DJ Kool Breez says. "We were like, 'Where is this dude?' And he wasn't calling us back, we were checking hospitals and shit."

Soon, Unruly's staff learned that the label's day-to-day operations were being relocated to DTLR's offices, and that the old team was being cut loose. "I didn't leave Unruly, they got rid of me," DJ Kool Breez says.

Even the Doo Dew Kidz, who'd produced a significant share of Unruly's most beloved tracks, were excluded from the new phase of Unruly, and decided to form their own label, DDK Records. "When Unruly started, it was a bunch of boys that were puttin' out music. And as it started makin' money, we were all young to the game, so we didn't know a lot of things about the business side," Booman recalls. "We went through a little split, then we sorta got back together, now everybody's cool. But it was just time for me and Griff and Jimmy to step out and do our own thing."

Booman and Jimmy Jones celebrated the genre they helped build on the second DDK release, which featured "Club Music Is My Life." It was another song on that EP, "Shout," featuring Jones hollering lyrics from the Isley Brothers classic of the same name, that eventually became a hit, but that took some work. "A lot of people were turnin' their backs on us, which we were like, 'What's going on?'" Jones told me in 2008. "We started hitting the ma 'n' pa venues, the bars and stuff like that, so we made a demand for people to want the record, because that's how we used to do it."

DJ Booman was also becoming as integral to the hip hop scene in Baltimore as he was to the club music scene. "I started in both genres, and I put an equal amount of energy into both," he says. Booman founded the rap label Crooked Streetz, and a collective of the same name, which included Jones, Pop Daddy, Lic Shots, Ant Boogie, Dragon, Point 4-5, and Trauma. Booman was one of the DJs in rotation on Baltimore's longest-running hip hop radio program, *Strictly Hip-Hop* on Morgan State's 88.9 WEAA. Crooked Streetz held a regular hip hop party at the Redwood Café in the late '90s, went on the road opening for major label rappers, and became a full-service entertainment company providing production, CD duplication, and T-shirt printing for independent artists in Baltimore.

Samir "Debonair Samir" Singletary, born in 1972, was another Baltimore club producer who was a lifelong disciple of hip hop. Growing up in New Jersey, he saw early hip hop pioneers spin in person. "Afrika Bambataa and Red Alert used to come to the projects where I used to live and DJ. So that's what made me wanna get into music, I was probably 6 or 7."

Debonair Samir began DJing and producing after moving to Baltimore in 1983, though he worked primarily in hip hop until Music Liberated owner Bernie Rabinowitz asked him to produce some club music for Baltimore Breakbeat Records in the late '90s. "He heard some of my stuff and asked me to remix a couple of songs," Samir says. "I'd always been into club music 'cause I was a dancer, back in the days when Unruly first started."

Samir's earliest club tracks didn't catch on, and he thinks that's because he wasn't following the simple, time-tested club music recipe. "The tracks I made in '98, I guess, were too different. You know how people are when they first get somethin' new, it's too off the wall."

A couple of years later, DJ Technics signed Debonair Samir to record for his Clubtrax Records label, which resulted in the songs that established Samir as a rising star on the scene. "I ran into Technics, and Technics gave me a deal and said, Okay, if you make these songs, I'll give you a certain amount of money," Samir remembers. Suitably incentivized, Samir went on a hot streak. "I made 40 club songs in two weeks."

That batch of tracks, including a remix of the Coasters' 1959 hit "Charlie Brown" and the South Park–sampling "Uncle Fucker," was also heavily inspired by Technics' influential "Dickontrol" kick-drum pattern. "I was like, 'Y'know what, I'll add the 'Dickontrol' beat, now everything's comin' to me.'" The relative simplicity of Baltimore club allowed Samir to focus and make the kind of impactful tracks that had evaded him as a rap producer. "I think about hip hop too hard, because now it's a billion-dollar business. When I'm makin' beats, I'm puttin' pressure on myself. When I'm makin' club music, I don't do that."

Debonair Samir named his best track after himself, though the title "Samir's Theme" actually wasn't his idea. "Technics named it, because we couldn't think of a name," Samir says. "I did not expect that song to go anywhere. That's the one that I'm gettin' comments from people around the world for."

Brass sounds played on synthesizers, not sampled from records with real horn sections, had been established as an appealing sound in Baltimore club music by the popularity of tracks like "Tear Da Club Up" and Rod Lee's "Feel Me." But "Samir's Theme" takes the crown for Baltimore club's most memorable synth horns, and it would be massively influential on the sound of 21st century club music. "Samir horns, that's a super classic," DJ Booman told host Chin-Yer Wright on the WEAA radio program *The Baltimore Scene* in June 2024.

Bernie Rabinowitz died in January 2003 in a car crash on the Jones Falls Expressway. He was driving home to Randallstown from one of the Music Liberated stores he'd been running for over 30 years. Rabinowitz had been such a fixture of the music retail business in Baltimore, since before the city even had DJs and dance clubs, that his passing represented the end of Baltimore club's golden age for many of the people he'd worked with.

In the late '90s and early 2000s, several DJs who'd been instrumental in the rise of club music moved, temporarily or permanently, to other parts of the country: Frank Ski to Atlanta, DJ Equalizer to Las Vegas, DJ Class to Atlanta, DJ Technics to North Carolina. But Debonair Samir was just one of many producers on the rise who would shape Baltimore club's growth as a genre and as a business in the coming years.

Chapter 12
Club Kings

Like Booman, Roderick Lee Sr. was the son of a musician. Both Rod Lee's father and his brother have been among the members of Panama Band, a Baltimore R&B combo that's been active for over 40 years, sharing stages with stars like Bobby Brown and the Stylistics. "I've always been around equipment, so I used to dabble with the drums, but I never took it serious," Lee says. "I just jumped straight into DJing. My old brother used to DJ first, and that's what made me wanna do it. We used to do house parties, actually it was rent parties, before I was a teenager."

Rod Lee started making records of his own simply as a strategy to get booked as a DJ. "I saw that I couldn't get a DJ gig in the clubs because, during that time, Reggie Reg and Mike Crosby and Rod Braxton and them, they had the clubs on lock, so you couldn't get any of those spots," Lee says. "So I was like, 'Fuck it, I'll just make the DJs come to me,' and I started making the music."

Rod Lee was only one year younger than Booman, but he was a relative late bloomer among the Baltimore club producers of his generation. Lee founded his own label, Phat Kidz Recordings, and his debut single, recorded in 1996, was "Rollin'." The record credits state, "Produced by DJ Rod Lee, engineered by Booman & DJ Rod Lee," but today Lee gives full credit to Booman for the "Sing Sing"–heavy beat.

"Booman produced that for me, I just did the vocals," Lee says.

Lee was a quick learner, though, building up his own home studio and self-producing his next release, "Bang That Thang." "I went straight from the blueprint I saw, Booman had showed it to me. The Sony DAT machine, you had to have that. Then the ASR, then you had to have the Mackie board, so you can put the meter bridge on it so you can separate the sounds," he says. "Once I got the ASR-10, I started just makin' club tracks, I had everything reserved. I had a hundred club tracks ready to come out."

Rod Lee's first DJ gig in a club in the mid-'90s was at the Federal Lounge in the Broadway East neighborhood, not far from where he lived. "K-Life got me that, because he would come over to my house and just watch me DJ, he'd be like, 'Yo, you nice, yo,'" Lee says. It didn't take him long to start drawing big crowds. "Saturday nights used to be packed, I turned that around in a month."

It was at the Federal Lounge that Lee met an ambitious teenage DJ who'd have a major impact on his career and the Baltimore club scene as a whole. Khia "DJ K-Swift" Edgerton, born in 1978, was still in high school, but she was already set on a music career. "K-Swift used to come and just sit at the bar. She was still too young to even get in the club, she'd just sit there and listen to the club music," Lee says. "I met her, she was like, 'I'ma DJ for you when I get older,' and I was like, 'Aight.'"

Rod Lee worked at Inner City Records and was intimately familiar with the burgeoning business of club music. "I always seen them making money from it, I always seen the records being sold off the wall. So I was like, shit, if they can do it, I can do it," he says. "Everything just went together hand in hand. The DJs was in the record stores, and the DJs made the records, so I just followed the plan of what I'd seen, I just mimicked it, that's all."

By the time Rod Lee got on a roll in the late '90s, he was quickly becoming the most prolific artist that Baltimore club music had ever seen, with much of his music released jointly by Phat Kidz and Knucklehead Records, the Unruly imprint run by DJ Technics. Lee was disrupting the established pace of club music release schedules, which ruffled some feathers. "I was like a cult going on at that time, like you only put one record out every month and all that," Lee says. "And I was like, 'Why?' They was like, 'Because you don't wanna saturate it,' I was like 'Why?' They was like, 'Yo, just don't do it.' And I did it because they told me don't do it."

DJ Technics and Rod Lee started a new label together, Club Kings. Lee likens them to Wolverine, the Marvel character who was a natural loner who didn't want to be part of the X-Men team (in this metaphor, Unruly Records). "We was Wolverine into the club music, because we weren't signed to other labels," he says. Technics was older and more established, and had a stronger claim to being the king, or a king, of Baltimore club. But Lee was quickly becoming massively popular in Baltimore, and they started to feel more like peers and equals. "We was puttin' out the hits at the time, so we were just like, 'Yo, we the club kings, fuck it.'"

When Technics eventually left Club Kings, moving to North Carolina for a few years, Lee kept the label going by himself, wearing the unofficial crown of the scene. "Little things would happen, and Tech didn't want no part of it, so he just walked away from it, and I kept the torch," Lee says.

Some of Rod Lee's hits were instrumental or only featured sampled vocals. At the time, setting a '50s or '60s R&B oldie to a Baltimore club beat was becoming a reliable formula. And Rod Lee would often pick samples based on what the musicians in his family had played when he was growing up. "Every Sunday, they would just bring the speakers out, the Fender amps, put the microphones up, and they just started singin'," he remembers. Shirley & Lee's 1956 hit "Let the Good Times Roll" was a particular favorite of his mother's, which he sampled on "C'mon Baby."

Rod Lee would occasionally get sued or threatened with lawsuits over samples, beginning with the Bohannon sample on one of his very first releases, "Bang That Thang." Usually he'd just shrug it off, confident that it wouldn't become a serious legal battle. "I knew you couldn't sue me, because nothin' from nothin' is nothin'. So by the time they lawyer up, you're payin' a lawyer more than it was worth suin' me. Once they see it's something independent, they say, 'We'll sit back, if it blow up, then we'll go at 'em,'" he says. "That's why we just started sampling anything we want to sample. Press five hundred records, a thousand records, who the hell's gonna sue you for that? It was funny to me, I didn't give a shit."

Eventually, though, for creative reasons, Rod Lee moved away from sampling to focus on tracks where he performed the vocals. Like Jimmy Jones or Miss Tony, Rod Lee is not a conventional singer or rapper, and his everyman bark only carries a little bit of melody. But his ear for catchy hooks was unparalleled, and he wrote full songs with verses, choruses, and bridges where previous Baltimore club vocalists would often repeat just one or a handful of lines for an entire track.

One of Rod Lee's most enduring songs was an intoxicating cocktail of Baltimore slang and a riff borrowed from the Eurodance scene, all the way on the opposite end of the dance music spectrum to Baltimore club. "I was down at the

Paradox, and I heard two motherfuckers sittin' there talking, and everything was, 'You feel me? You feel what I'm sayin'?' I'm sittin' in the house and see the Six Flags Great Adventure commercial." The popular amusement park's ad campaign, featuring the Dutch group Vengaboys' 1998 hit "We Like to Party," inspired the synth horn riff on Rod Lee's wildly popular track "Feel Me."

"Everybody was samplin' records so much, and I just got tired of that, sample sample sample," Lee says. "I said, 'I ain't samplin' no more. I'm just usin' my own vocals.' So I started my own trend." Lee's hits, featuring his own original lyrics and melodies, started piling up: "Mind Ya Business," "Birthday," "Understand," "25 & Older," "Bombin' Bitch," "Hi-Man," "Creep Tonight," and on and on and on.

"I know what part of the record that can get you jumpin'," Lee says. "So when I put my EPs together, I know what's the hit on the record, or what's the two hits on the record, that determines how much I'ma charge you for the record."

Rjyan Kidwell was a White teenager in Baltimore's indie rock scene in the late '90s who'd become enamored with dance music and began releasing music under the name Cex. Cex became associated with the questionably-named genre IDM ("intelligent dance music"), but he loved more physical, danceable styles of music, particularly Baltimore club, and Rod Lee was one of his favorite producers.

Kidwell delighted in playing songs like "Feel Me" in front of White hipsters.

"The first reaction playing that track for someone who never heard club was alway, 'Are you kidding me?' which slowly turned into 'What even is this?', and then once the fake brass stabs kick in, you could see their whole idea of the world get bigger. Jaws would drop to the floor and anybody except the most macho emcees were invariably using the word 'genius' and demanding you burn them a copy."

As competitive as the Baltimore club market was, it was a tightly knit community of producers who respected each other, played each other's music, and were motivated by each other's success. "Booman would call me, 'Yo, I got some tracks for you,' and I would buy tracks from Booman to put em on Club Kingz. It's like everybody doin' their own thing but we never beef, we all got along," Lee says. "So Booman puts something out, and I call him, I say, 'You motherfucker, I'ma get you.' Booman starts laughing. But I come back, and then Griff'll come out, Dukeyman will come out with something. It's always, 'Yo, you heard it yet?'"

A few years after meeting at the Federal Lounge, Rod Lee and DJ K-Swift were both fast-rising stars in Baltimore, and she'd begun to DJ on the radio, working for 92Q (92.3 WERQ). But K-Swift was in a bad contract with Troy Brown of the Baltimore club production team Wax Musicians, and asked for Lee's help. Brown claimed that he owned the name "DJ K-Swift" and served cease-and-desist letters demanding that she stop using her DJ name on the radio.

"I said, 'Alright, we're gonna do it like this, we're gonna change the name,'" Lee says. "Swift was like, 'No! My name!' I said, 'Now just rock with me, I'm the Club King, you the Club Queen. And she was like, 'Yo! I like that!' I said alright, so no more K-Swift. And from that day on, she never said K-Swift no more, she said, 'It's your girl, the Club Queen.'"

Then Lee bought out K-Swift's contract with Troy Brown and signed her to Club Kings. "I gave him double what he asked for, shook his hand, and that was that," Lee says. "The contract was a couple grand, it wasn't nothin' big, but during that time, she really didn't know what she was doing. I bought it, and I just tore it up." She was able to use her old name again, but she kept her new title: now she was K-Swift the Club Queen.

K-Swift would play Rod Lee's music heavily on 92Q, and she'd get new exclusive tracks from him before anybody else – he even custom-made tracks for her to use as a music bed when she was speaking on the air. "It was just loops that I made for Swift, when she would go on break and started talking, so she always needed instrumentals. So I just started makin' 'em, and then as she started playin' 'em, I just started puttin' 'em on the EPs as fillers," he says. One of those beats, "Nutty Track," took off and became a hit in clubs.

The 1998 single "Baltimore Things," credited to World Premiere, featured Johnny "Porkchop" Doswell of Da Horsemen rapping over a Rod Lee beat. "Pork was my first artist," Lee said. "Baltimore Things" didn't make big waves, though it's endured as a minor local classic, and K.W. Griff sampled Porkchop's voice from the song for a club music staple, 2006's "Ain't None O' Y'all Safe." And Lee's next collaboration with a rapper would set the standard for fusions of Baltimore club music and hip hop.

Wayne Jones III started rapping under the name Tim Trees as a teenager, forming the group Bdamore Murdaland with his cousin T-Rock. After T-Rock went to jail in 1997, Tim Trees went solo, with the group becoming the namesake of the label Bdamore Records, run by his friends Dwight "Manny" Barlow and Andre Williams.

Barlow reached out to Rod Lee in 2000 to produce the first Tim Trees album, but he didn't want Baltimore club beats. "Manny come down in my basement, he's like, 'Yo, you need to stop playing all that club shit, and make some real shit. And when he said it, it just made me upset," Lee says. So he took the sample he'd been working on for a club track, a single bass note from a Dionne Warwick record, slowed down the tempo, and made it into a throbbing, stuttering pulse over a loping 93 BPM beat.

Tim Trees wrote boastful, aspirational punchlines over Rod Lee's beat – like "My necklace got me a nickname, treasure chest" – in his grandmother's house. And the song "Bank Roll" made him into the star he claimed to be in its lyrics, a classic hip hop story of turning nothing into something. Tim Trees played the song for people in his neighborhood. "When we let 'em hear 'Bank Roll,' they just went crazy. It was undeniable," Tim Trees says.

At that point, though, most of the local music that got played on Baltimore radio was club music, and very few rappers had broken through, so "Bank Roll" faced some resistance at 92Q. "The DJs wouldn't play it, they would play the beat only," Lee says. Bdamore Records wasn't happy with the situation, and tried to use physical force to make the song a hit. "Wasn't nobody playin' it, but then Manny and them, they just started goin' around beatin' the DJs up. They beat up damn near everybody back in the day who weren't playing their record. They thought I had somethin' to do with it too. I said, 'I ain't touch nobody!'"

"Bank Roll" finally took off when Rod Lee was hired by 92Q in November 2000. On a typical hip hop radio station in another city, there might be serious issues with a recording artist or producer playing and promoting their own music on the air. In Baltimore, however, club music was such a small and collaborative scene that it would've been almost impossible for a station like 92Q to play Baltimore club without having the genre's top artists DJing on the air.

The follow-up to "Bank Roll" was another huge local hit, "We Don't Love 'Em," which featured a slower version of a drum pattern Rod Lee used on the club track "The Bernie Mack Theme."

"Without Manny, it wouldn't be no Tim Trees," Lee says. "Promotion-wise, everything, really went out in the street, out his trunk. He would walk to your car while you were at the light, and was like, 'You don't know Tim Trees? You need to buy one of these,' and then people would just all buy it."

Tim Trees frequently referred to himself on record by his real name, Wayne Jones, or as Timothy Dalton, a reference to the British actor who played James Bond in the 1980s. Lee produced the bulk of the first Tim Trees album, 2001's *Dalton, Vol. 1*, which sold over ten thousand copies, as well as the follow-up, 2002's *Dalton, Vol. 2*. After that, however, Rod Lee's price went up to produce for rappers and singers. "I was charging fifteen thousand dollars a track."

Local rappers were happy to pay Rod Lee's asking price, and more hits followed, like "Shake It Shorty" by the group Nature's Problem, and "They Call me Clayway" by Little Clayway. Rod Lee produced local R&B hits like Davon's 2002 hit "Be Ya Friend" and Paula Campbell's 2003 hit "How Does It Feel" – both of which featured guest verses by Tim Trees – and later, "Turn It Down" by RuScola, a member of Dru Hill.

Debonair Samir, who had spent some time back in New Jersey and New York after his unsuccessful early attempts at Baltimore club tracks, was newly inspired when he returned to Baltimore and heard what Rod Lee was doing. "When I moved back here in 2001, I heard the Tim Trees joint and the Porkchop joint and I was like, 'Man this is a sound!'"

Dukeyman had produced four tracks on *Dalton, Vol. 1*, but Tim Trees had passed on a Dukeyman beat that sampled "Movin' On Up," the theme song to the '70s sitcom *The*

Jeffersons. Dukeyman offered the track to Brian Rich, who rapped under the name B. Rich. B. Rich made "Whoa Now" over the bouncy, handclap-driven track with a rubbery, singsong melodic flow that was closer to Nelly than Tim Trees's gruff, grimy delivery, and the cheerful, nostalgic sample made it sound even more mainstream-friendly.

The original "Whoa Now" that dominated Baltimore radio still had a slightly rough, lo-fi Baltimore club aesthetic to it. Within a matter of months, though, Atlantic Records signed B. Rich and had Dukeyman make a more polished version of the track that became a national hit in the summer of 2002. "Whoa Now" just barely made the Hot 100 for two weeks, peaking at #98, but did better on *Billboard*'s hip hop charts, gaining national radio airplay.

For a brief, unprecedented moment in 2002, there were two music videos in rotation on MTV and BET that featured Baltimore natives showing off their city: "Whoa Now" and teen R&B singer Mario's debut single, "Just A Friend 2002," an update of a Biz Markie hit from the late '80s. Dukeyman produced the bulk of B. Rich's Atlantic album *80 Dimes*, but tapped into his substantial skillset as a more conventional hip hop producer for the other tracks. Lukasz "Dr. Luke" Gottwald, who would begin producing a huge number of chart-topping pop hits within the next couple of years, contributed one beat to *80 Dimes*, which peaked at #100 on the *Billboard* 200 album chart. B. Rich was dismissed by many as a one-hit wonder before he'd even released a follow-up single. What little mainstream press B. Rich received gave no cultural context for the Baltimore club scene that the song and its producer emerged from.

When I met Dukeyman a few years later in 2006, he seemed unphased by B. Rich's brief moment of national stardom, disappointed but not surprised that the label rushed the album out without a long-term plan. "It ain't get a lot of promotion. We're on tour while they're [finalizing] the album, we didn't get a chance to do no photo shoot for the album cover," he said. "It was just another stepping stone for me, really. Just another new experience. Y'know, at the time, that's what you wish for, but when you see how it really is, it ain't all it's cracked up to be."

Paula Campbell became a local star after the release of "How Does It Feel," and performed at many 92Q events and opened for major touring artists. Rod Lee produced intro music for her stage show that centered on the "Think (About It)" breakbeat, dramatically slowed down to 90 BPM, far slower than even the Lyn Collins original, with a droning synth horn riff.

In 2004, Travis "Bossman" Davon of the Baltimore hip hop group North East Kings walked into Rod Lee's Club Kingz record store on Monument Street to ask for that track. "I actually heard that beat in the intro for Paula Campbell," Bossman says. "I would say, 'Yo, gimme the beat that you played for the intro at that show.'"

The song they made over that beat, "Oh," was Bossman's first solo single, a huge regional hit and hometown anthem for Baltimore. Bossman, who patterned his writing style on erudite New York rappers like Nas and Jadakiss, brought a different energy to Rod Lee's production than the more playful style of Tim Trees or Nature's Problem. "At heart, I'm a lyricist, but Rod's type of thing, the two step, it needs to be a combination," says Bossman.

"The way he rap, he's impeccable, that's like my favorite rapper," says Lee.

Paula Campbell signed to Sony and Bossman signed to

Virgin Records, both largely off the strength of regional radio play for the songs Rod Lee produced. Neither of them ever got to release a major-label album like B. Rich, though, and neither released much more music with Rod Lee – Bossman and Rod Lee's second song together, a mixtape track called "Let's Go," was held back from an official release when a Slick Rick sample couldn't get cleared.

After club music had been ignored by the music industry for a decade, major labels were starting to take an interest in the Baltimore sound, particularly Rod Lee's version of it. "I was livin' on Kenwood and Monument, that's where all the hits was coming out of, on Kenwood. Everybody I ever recorded, that was the hit factory. Paula Campbell, RuScola, Tim Trees, Bossman, Porkchop, Nature's Problem," says Lee.

The Neptunes, the Virginia Beach production team of Pharrell Williams and Chad Hugo, were doing what Rod Lee was doing on a much larger mainstream level, producing dozens of international chart hits for Jay-Z, Nelly, Ludacris, and others. Baltimore club music's regional following extended down to southern Virginia at that point, and Williams was a vocal fan.

Lee remembers that even in the '90s, his label's distributor, Liaison, kept him up to speed on his growing following in Virginia. "It was that easy, thanks to Liaison. Tom [Goldfogle] and Becky [Marcus] and them. They bridged the gap with us, like, 'DJ such-and-such in Richmond wanna holla at you.'"

One day in the early 2000s, Reggie Reg was on the air on 92Q and put out an urgent message to one of his co-workers: "Rod Lee, call the station if you're listenin', call the radio station!"

Rod Lee was in his car when his phone rang. "My girl called

me, and she said, 'They're telling you to call the radio station, Pharrell's up in here.'"

Pharrell Williams was telling everyone at the station that he wanted to sign Rod Lee to his label. Lee called the station, but he wasn't especially receptive to the superstar producer's offer. "I said, 'What's up, guy?' and we got to rappin' a little bit. But at the time, man, I was in the street. I didn't care about the money part," Lee says. Williams threw around some big financial figures, but Lee was unmoved, as he was already making that kind of money in Baltimore as an independent artist, label owner, producer, DJ, record store proprietor, and radio personality. "In my mind, I'm like, 'I've got that in my pocket now, what are you talkin' about?'"

"I ain't makin' millions of dollars, but I can say I'm one of the ones out of Baltimore that made more money than anybody here off of club music," Lee says.

In retrospect, Lee thinks he probably should've listened to Pharrell Williams. But he was his own boss, and nobody was there to advise him to go into business with Williams, who has remained a major celebrity and hitmaker in the decades since. "Had I known what I know now, I woulda did it, I would've signed, if I had somebody during that time that was more on the manager side, like, 'Yo, take the less money, you're gonna get bigger exposure,'" Lee says. "Wasn't nobody in my ear tellin' me that. I was like, 'Nah, I ain't doin' that shit.'"

In 2007, Rod Lee got another call from a friend who was in London, where Williams was DJing at a Louis Vuitton fashion show and playing Baltimore club tracks while models strutted on the catwalk. Williams played tracks by Rod Lee, DJ Technics, and DJ Ron Rico, telling the audience, "I'm getting' ready to introduce this new sound!"

A few months later, Williams gave an interview to MTV News to explain that "Give It Up," the new single he'd produced for Chicago rap star Twista, was his homage to Baltimore. "Baltimore house is incredible," said Williams. "For 20 years, that Baltimore stuff has been, like, insane and banging. I wanted to give my own interpretation of it, which is a little bit of Miami, a little of Baltimore house."

At 122 BPM, "Give It Up" was a little slow for Baltimore club, and without breakbeats, it sounded more like a lot of other Pharrell Williams productions of the era, with heavily reverbed live drum sounds and organ riffs. It wasn't much of a commercial success either, stalling at #88 on *Billboard*'s Hot R&B/Hip-Hop Songs chart and missing the Hot 100. I asked Rod Lee if he'd heard the Twista song. "Yup, and it got booed."

Chapter 13
Tote It

Khia Edgerton, the eldest child of Joseph and Juanita Edgerton, grew up in Randallstown, one of the most predominantly Black suburbs in Baltimore County. She got her first turntables at 15, spinning records for friends in her basement and at local house parties. As a teenager she idolized Spinderella, the trailblazing female DJ who rose to fame performing with Salt-N-Pepa. "She was like a sponge when it came to music," Joseph Edgerton told the *Baltimore Sun*.

A couple of years after Edgerton told Rod Lee about her ambitions to become a club music DJ, she made her debut at the Arbutus club Twilight Zone, owned by Jimmy Trujillo. DJ Spice, who also worked at the club, was in the house on April 20, 1997, and captured video footage of DJ K-Swift spinning K.W. Griff and DJ Booman's "Pick 'Em Up." "I was less than a year into my residency at Twilight Zone in Baltimore, MD, when Jimmy T decided to give this girl Khia Edgerton a chance to spin," DJ Spice wrote when posting the video on YouTube in 2016. "She immediately had the crowd rockin, so I picked up my video camera and caught a few minutes."

Twilight Zone, which operated from 1995 to 1998, was K-Swift's launching pad, and where she met many of the DJs, hosts, and promoters who'd remain in her circle for the next decade and eventually join her Club Queen Entertainment team: Buck Jones, DJ Lucky, Lady Pitbull, and two founding members of Da Horsemen, Johnny "Porkchop" Doswell and Supa DJ Big L.

Some Baltimore club DJs would get on the mic and hype up the crowd and do shout outs while spinning, but there was often a party host who would handle those duties. Buck Jones is one of club music's most seasoned party hosts, and he manned the microphone for K-Swift's sets from very early on in her career. Jones remembers that K-Swift struggled for recognition, and endured chauvinistic doubts about her musical abilities as a woman. "Every week she would say to me, 'Make sure you pump my name up,' because a lot of people would have this impression that she wasn't mixin'," Jones says.

"A female in the entertainment business just gets looked over," Lady Pitbull says.

"Me, Buck, Lucky, and Big L was workin' for the club, so it started there. And when she said, 'Let's do the Club Queen Entertainment thing from there,' when Swift first got her own money and threw the parties herself, we was all in there. We might not have been gettin' paid, but we all was there, and everybody saw it come together," says Porkchop, who also became the director of K-Swift's record pool. "She fed us, clothed us. She was so like the mother of all of us, even though we're probably all older than her, which I'll never get. She was just the big sister, big mother of everybody."

Trujillo also kickstarted K-Swift's radio career, helping her get an internship at 92Q that would eventually lead to her spinning on the air and becoming one of the station's most popular personalities. She had been overweight as a teenager, and as her profile rose, she got more health-conscious. She lost 175 pounds thanks to a soup-heavy diet, vitamin B12 injections, and a program at the Extreme Weight Loss Center in Windsor Mill. "When she got small, she was already larger than life," DJ Lucky says.

K-Swift had taken classes at Community College of Baltimore County, Catonsville, and one of the other students she befriended there, rapper Kevin "Ogun" Beasley, would also become an influential mainstay of Baltimore's music scene. "I can truthfully say she knew exactly who she would become," Ogun says.

> "She knew that she could become the best female DJ in the city, and then the world. Now, you gotta think, this is before her major makeover and loss of weight. So the confidence she projected was so obvious and contagious, I just knew she was going to accomplish all her dreams."

Reginald "Reggie Reg" Calhoun, born in 1965, had been DJing in Baltimore since the Odell's era, and was one of 92Q's most recognizable voices. And he was integral in making both K-Swift and Rod Lee into popular on-air personalities. "He gave me my start at the radio station," says Lee, who collaborated with Reggie Reg on the song "Club Face." Most of Baltimore was introduced to K-Swift as Reggie Reg's co-host on *Off the Hook Radio*, where they had a friendly, big brother/little sister on-air dynamic. Eventually, she'd take over as the nightly show's primary host.

K-Swift loved to play card games like spades with her friends in her Randallstown apartment. When her career started to become lucrative, she'd take weekend trips to Atlantic City, New Jersey and Dover, Delaware casinos, and would often leave with more money than she came with. "Man, she was a genius in Atlantic City," says Porkchop. "She could go there back-to-back weekends, come back with twenty-four thousand, eighteen thousand, killin' it."

Rod Lee was the first popular producer who gave K-Swift his new tracks before anybody else, but soon many more were giving her exclusives. "The only person that got it was Swift. So all the DJs was glued to listen to what she gonna play on Saturday nights and go down to Bernie's store next week and look for what she played," Lee says.

Most of the key DJs and producers in Baltimore club up to that point had been born in the late '60s and early '70s. But K-Swift, who was born in the late '70s, was a key transitional figure who opened the door for a new generation. She helped popularize the first wave of Baltimore club producers born in the '80s, many of whom started making beats on DAWs (digital audio workstations, as in software programs that ran on laptops), instead of the ASR-10. "Think (About It)," "Sing Sing," and other breakbeats were still in the mix, but the sound of club music was changing, featuring more synths and drum machines, and even gradually reaching into faster tempos. The analog feel of early Baltimore club was givig way to a more overtly digital aesthetic.

Brandon "Say Wut" Tennessee, born in 1982, was just a teenager when he joined one of the later iterations of Da Horsemen. "Brandon and I go back probably further than most, because Brandon's brother and I worked together as kids. So I've known Brandon for many years, he's younger than me, but I've known his family," Diamond K says.

By the time Da Horsemen's original run was winding down, Say Wut had taken an interest in making his own tracks, and asked for guidance from Dukeyman, who'd co-produced many of the group's songs. "I was just graduatin' from high school, I didn't have no money for no MPC2000 or ASR keyboard or anything like that. So I said, 'Alright, Dukeyman, I need to try this on my own.'" He started making tracks on FruityLoops, then Reason, and eventually getting proper studio equipment.

Say Wut joined the Club Queen team, as did his girlfriend and future wife Crystal Briscoe (now Crystal Tennessee). "Darven [Cook], Say Wut, and me basically ran her street team," says Crystal Tennesee. "The way that we did it, we would recruit high school kids to work for us, and they would get in for free. So they thought that was the coolest thing, to be on Swift's list."

Some Baltimore club parties were 21-and-up, but K-Swift made it increasingly profitable to welcome teens into the clubs for 17-and-over or 18-and-over parties. "Everybody got outta school the same time," Porkchop said, laying out their strategy for distributing flyers at the biggest high schools in the city to spread the word. "The week of the party, we would do Edmondson, Carver, and Walbrook, then do Mervo, City College, and try to go to every school."

Sometimes K-Swift herself would make appearances at the schools, where she was greeted as a hometown hero. "I have never walked into a high school gym and seen people go crazy like that," DJ Lucky says.

When Say Wut began making tracks, he named his production company Horsemen Entertainment, a nod to the group he started with. But Diamond K had never stopped releasing music under the banner of Da Horsemen, and a later lineup of the group released the 2008 album *HWO Revolution*. "When he did Horsemen Ent., it definitely rubbed me the wrong way," Diamond K says. "Best believe I was pissed!" he adds with a self-deprecating laugh.

Say Wut started to become one of the most popular producers in the city after being heavily featured in K-Swift's radio sets, and she became his manager. "Hornz Theme," also known as "Hornz Joint," sampled Debonair Samir's "Samir's Theme" and ramped up the intensity, making synth horns a staple of tracks by Say Wut and many of the younger producers that came up in his wake.

"There was, like, this new wave of club goin' on now. So I started doin' a little experimenting here and there and, I'm not gonna say 'created,' but contributed to a new sound that's starting to evolve," Say Wut told me the first time I met him, in 2006.

In the early 2000s, producer tags became trendy in hip hop, a quick audio stamp that would announce who made the beat even if the song was credited to a rapper. Baltimore club producers still sometimes had trouble achieving name recognition in the city, but Say Wut's producer tag helped him become a recognizable brand. "I was like, man, nobody really knows who I am, I need to put my name in a song or something," Say Wut says. "I was sittin' there thinkin' that, got on the mic, and said, 's-s-s-Say Wuuut,'" he adds, stuttering and elongating his name as in the famous sound bite that began opening many of his tracks.

Charles Jamal Smith, born in 1985, fell in love with DJing in the late '90s. "When I first started out, I had one crate, and half of the crate was hip hop, and half of the crate was club music," says Smith. "That was my life, that's how I made my living. It was music, renting sound [equipment], DJing. And making tracks was just a hobby, it was moreso a promotional tool back then, to help me get my name out there."

When Smith began producing tracks under the name Blaqstarr, though, he quickly proved to be a true original, one of the most creative producers ever to come out of the Baltimore club scene. He had his own producer tag ("Blaqstarr, break it down"), but it wasn't as necessary for him as for others, because his beats and his voice were so distinctive.

One of the first songs Blaqstarr sent to K-Swift, when he was just 18 years old, was "Tote It," a revolutionary track that abandoned breakbeats and synthesizers in favor of a pulsing kick drum, booming shotgun sound effects, and Blaqstarr's high and haunting, almost androgynous voice mixed with a cacophony of vocal loops, including Georgia rapper Bone Crusher's voice from his 2003 hit "Never Scared." Whether or not she realized how different it was from the other tracks in her sets, K-Swift put "Tote It" on the radio, and the reaction was immediate. "I gave her a couple tracks, she played them, and I started gettin' known," Blaqstarr says.

Like most Baltimore club producers who performed vocals on their own tracks, Blaqstarr was not a master singer in a conventional sense, but he had an incredible gift for melody and a unique voice that people loved to listen to. His vocals sounded nothing like the raspy, gregarious club chants on a Jimmy Jones or Rod Lee track, but he also didn't sound like anyone outside Baltimore. "I used to sing real serious, in front of girls back in high school," he says. The lyrics to "Tote It" were not exactly romantic, though: "I told y'all I tote it/ put the bullet in the Glock and blowed it."

An even bigger song, "Get My Gun" – with the refrain "You keep on fuckin' around, I'm gon' go get my gun" – followed a similar formula, but had such an infectious melody that it felt like anything but a serious gangsta rap pose. Blaqstarr's tracks were layered and left-field compared to most of the Baltimore club music that preceded him, but when a track would pull away those layers, he could destroy dancefloors with just a simple bass-drum pattern and a vocal hook. "The kick was doin' so much to 'em," Blaqstarr says with pride.

When I met Blaqstarr for the first time, in a Panera Bread in Towson, a couple of years after those songs took off, he was a skinny kid barely out of his teens. He brought along his brother Joe "J-Beezy" Smith, whom he frequently collaborated with under the name Starr Productions. "I'll write some stuff and some of the stuff he writes," J-Beezy said. Blaqstarr gave me his 2006 mix CD *I'm Banging*, a remarkable half-hour showcase of most of the tracks that had conquered Baltimore over the previous couple of years, including some gems that never made it onto the internet.

Even then, Blaqstarr came off as a soft-spoken but confident young guy who could be hard to pin down. He told me that his real name was "Jamal Starr" (it is not). His fashion sense was a little bohemian, but it was the enigmatic, somewhat evasive way he thought and spoke that made him seem like a true eccentric. Talking to him was what I imagine what it would've been like to interview a young Prince or David Bowie.

Just as '90s Baltimore producers often found that the more aggressive and animated voices like Busta Rhymes or Onyx sounded great on club tracks, mid-2000s producers favored Lil Jon. There was no voice in rap that was louder and more over-the-top at the time than Lil Jon, the Atlanta producer who became the face of a southern rap subgenre called crunk, which had roots in Miami bass. Lil Jon's trademark screams ("what," "yeah," "okay") became a staple of crunk, and soon enough Lil Jon samples were inescapable in Baltimore club. Younger producers like Say Wut who were pushing the energy higher with blaring synths found that a well-placed Lil Jon scream could always kick things up another notch, a stuttering "what" loop playing patterns like a hi-hat.

Mike "DJ Mic Marvelous" McLean, born in 1983, started out with a stint with Say Wut's Horsemen Entertainment. Mic

Marvelous hit his stride in the Lil Jo–sample era of Baltimore club music, with his co-productions with DJ Twikks becoming a staple of K-Swift's *Jumpoff* mixtape series. On "Let the Bodies Hit the Floor," Mic Marvelous tried out an unlikely sample: the menacing whispers from the nu-metal band Drowning Pool's 2001 hit "Bodies."

Mic Marvelous's first attempt at the track retained the loud guitar-driven sections of the Drowning Pool song, but he faced resistance from Baltimore crowds when he played the early version. "I tested it out in the club, and I got this crazy-ass look like, 'What the hell is he playin'?'" he says. Fortunately, those reliable Lil Jon screams were there to help make his unorthodox sample more palatable. "I changed it and stuck the Lil Jon in there and they loved it. What I try to do is incorporate different sounds. I love that different type of feelin'. If they're not used to it, get 'em used to it."

Chapter 14
The 9 O'Clock Mix

In the early days, Baltimore club DJs often made their own mixtapes and sold them on cassette at gigs, a side hustle that could bring in more money than the gig itself. "I did parties for 40 dollars, man," Brownlee says.

"And me and DJ Paradise, we would get the 40 dollars, we would go down to the Chinese store. We would buy a brick of tapes, like 20 tapes, and we'd buy 2 masters, like a metal Maxell, to make the master copy, and we would copy the tapes."

According to DJ Booman and K.W. Griff, mixtapes demonstrated an early geographic difference in the club music scene: DJs from West Baltimore tended to talk over their tracks, and do chants and shoutouts on their tapes, while East Baltimore DJs like the Doo Dew Kidz were, at least at first, strictly letting the music do the talking.

Scottie B. was part of the West Baltimore faction. His mixtapes were particularly popular, but he wasn't able to sell them at Inner City Records at first, because they didn't have barcodes like a mass-produced release from a proper label. So Scottie would work the counter at the store but send Brownlee down to Lexington Market to sell his tapes at 10 dollars a pop. "Bein' around him was like I was with a dope dealer, but we were selling music," Brownlee says. "And it felt good, it felt fuckin' good, man. You understand what I'm sayin'? People was happy."

A few years later, the music retailers got in on the mixtape business, but had to get creative to keep up with demand. "My funniest memory of Equalizer, we're selling mixtapes, and we have a machine called a Telex machine we'd use to duplicate the tapes," Diamond K says.

> "And it would duplicate both sides of a cassette tape in like two minutes, y'know, high speed. And sometimes we would run out of a particular tape somebody wants. So they're comin' in the store, they're shopping, 'Okay, give me the latest club tape,' and sometimes we'd run out. And what he would do sometimes, is he would sell a blank tape as if it was the mix. And then he would say, 'Well, when they bring it back, we'll give 'em one and say it was a defective. Just get the money.'"

By the end of the '90s, though, compact disc duplicating was becoming more accessible and affordable, and CDs quickly became the most popular format for Baltimore club mixes. The mix CDs, increasingly, tended to be more polished and consumer-friendly than the cassette versions, with promotional rollouts like albums. DJs loved making them, although the subject of who would get to release mixes through Unruly became contentious. "It started bein' a headache because everyone wanted to do one, 'Well you got them and not me,' blah blah," Scottie B. says ruefully.

The Baltimore club community had long thrived on the fact that everyone in the scene would play each other's music, that the allegiances or rivalries between different labels or cliques were secondary to the need to play the hottest songs. When Rod Lee opened his first Club Kingz store, he'd readily sell other artists' music, often releasing it on his label as well. "I had everybody's stuff, then I started puttin' out greatest hits, Club Kingz greatest hits, Blaqstarr, Patrick, everybody."

"We all was cool," Dukeyman told me in 2008.

"So if Rod Lee said, 'Yo, make me a couple tracks, put em on my album,' cool, I slipped him a joint. Me and Technics did an album. We swap out tracks, everybody just helpin' each other get money, just puttin' their little two cents in. Not sayin' they couldn't sit there and make their own whole album, but everybody makes tracks differently."

But as mix CDs entered the picture, DJs and producers became a little more selective and possessive about who they would put on their CDs and whether they were okay with someone else putting their music on a CD.

"That was tough, just because you wanna use other people's shit too, and then they beef about it," Scottie B. says. It was also difficult for Unruly to control whether their mix CDs were competing with other independently sold mix CDs by the same DJs. "You gotta tell 'em, 'You gotta pull all your stuff off the street when this is out,' and they ain't wanna do it, because they want money comin' in their pocket."

There had never been much exclusivity in Baltimore club, whether in label deals, club engagements, or the sharing of songs and samples. The mixtape game made things a little more territorial and hostile. It was a change from the vinyl-driven days of club music, when producers were sharing white labels of new tracks with their favorite DJs and proudly hanging them up on the display walls of record stores in the hopes that every other club DJ in town would pick up a couple of copies. There were now more producers with more music entering the marketplace, but it was harder to profit from it, making them a more intensely protected resource.

Reggie Reg's Unruly mix CDs *Feel Me* and *The 9 O'Clock Mix* were highly popular, particularly because of his radio platform on 92Q. Rico "DJ Quicksilva" Silva, born in 1980, was a charismatic teenager who'd been working in the local clubs from a young age, and grew up in the same neighborhood as DJ Booman and K.W. Griff. DJ Quicksilva took over the Unruly Record Pool after DJ Kool Breez was let go, and Quicksilva's mix CDs quickly made him a highly visible new part of the Unruly team.

Rod Lee released his first Club Kingz mix CD, *Operation: Start-Up*, in 2001, and followed it annually with sequels over the next few years – *Vol. 2: Operation Not Done Yet*, *Vol. 3: Operation Shut Em Down*, and *Vol. 4: The Pressure*. Although Rod Lee would sprinkle in tracks by other artists, he was virtually the only Baltimore club producer who was prolific enough to regularly make 60-minute mixes composed primarily of his own tracks. And since vinyl was still selling at that point, the popularity of his mixtapes also helped market his records.

"When I got into the CD game, it changed everything for me, because I'm used to sellin' vinyl," Rod Lee says.

"So I just price-jacked the vinyl too, it was 25 dollars for six tracks. They was like, 'Who the hell Rod Lee think he is?' But when [K-Swift] played it on the radio, we made a demand of it, so that's what people wanted to hear when they went to the clubs, they wanted to hear what they heard on the radio."

As a one-man hit factory, Lee was competitive with the entire rosters of other labels, and he had the business savvy to capitalize on his prolific output. "You've just gotta know how to market your music," he says. "You gotta look at it independently, locally, you're only gonna get but so much. You gotta put a cap on it. Like for my mix CD, I said, 'I wanna make ten grand.' So out of that, I done it, I'm on to the next thing now."

K-Swift's *Club Queen* series was her marquee mix CD franchise, with the highly popular *Jumpoff* series kicking off in 2004. With her audience skewing younger and younger as her fame grew, she began another series, *Strictly For The Kids*, with a family-friendly selection of club music with no swear words and lots of samples from cartoons. Its counterpart, the *Strictly For Tha Streets* series, featured more aggressive club tracks with more samples of contemporary rap hits. All in all, K-Swift was averaging a new mix CD about every three months, if not even more often.

In the vinyl era, photos of Baltimore club producers and artists rarely appeared on record sleeves, and fans of their music might have no idea what they looked like unless they saw them DJ in person. But with Rod Lee and K-Swift appearing on the covers of their mix CDs, they were quickly becoming local celebrities in a way that only Frank Ski and Miss Tony had achieved in earlier eras of club music.

One day in 2005, I called the phone number on the cover of a *Jumpoff* CD to order a new volume of the series. I expected to leave a voicemail, or speak to one of K-Swift's employees, and was a little starstruck when I heard the same voice speaking to me that I'd heard on the radio nearly every day. My writing career had barely started at that point, and I later assumed I'd eventually meet K-Swift in person and interview her, but that was the only time I ever spoke to her.

In Tierre Brownlee's view, the mix-CD era had an overall negative effect on relationships within the scene, and strained the established system by which songs spread around to different DJs and clubs and became hits. "I'ma tell you what killed Baltimore club music. When certain people was gettin' tracks, and they would put 'em on CDs," he says.

"Then you had the Rod Lees, then you had the K-Swifts, their stuff was comin' out on CD, that was, like, exclusive, you had to be in a certain echelon of the music in Baltimore to get they shit. And that's when dudes get the CDs and snipin' off CDs, you know what I mean, little parts of records, that's what sorta killed Baltimore club music."

Lesser-known DJs would put together mixes cobbled together from the excerpts of hot new songs that had been premiered on mixes by the big-name DJs. In addition to the scene becoming more divided and stratified, the sound quality of the mixes sometimes suffered due to these methods, as well as the digital compression of songs sometimes traded as MP3 files.

After K-Swift's earlier deals with Troy Brown, Rod Lee, and others, she eventually aligned with Unruly Records, who had been courting her for years. "It took several attempts," says Scottie B. He may have had mixed feelings (no pun intended) about focusing on mix CDs over vinyl, but selling K-Swift mixes at Downtown Locker Room stores was a highly profitable proposition for both parties.

"It was kinda like people lost her more than we gained her," Scottie B. says.

"She was with somebody, she moved onto somebody else, she moved onto somebody else, she moved onto somebody else, because they kept tryin' to do dumb stuff. Eventually the next-biggest person did something, I don't know what, and then it was like, 'Well, we're the only ones left, what you wanna do?'"

In 2005, K-Swift released the sixth installment in her *Club Queen* series, *Vol. 6: The Return.* It was her first release through Unruly, and her first CD released in a traditional jewelcase, not a slim mixtape case. It featured era-defining tracks from the producers she worked the most closely with, like Blaqstarr's "Get My Gun" and Say Wut's "Hornz Theme."

Mix CDs and 92Q made Baltimore club music accessible in a way it hadn't been in the '90s, especially to teenagers. Instead of selling vinyl primarily to DJs, labels were now selling CDs to fans of all ages, who might have heard the music on the radio without ever stepping foot in the Paradox or Hammerjacks. Some older DJs didn't necessarily think the music should've crossed over to mainstream broadcasts, however. "Club music was made for clubs, very provocative and nasty and perverted," Dukeyman told me in 2006. "There's a reason why it was called club music, because you have to go to the club to listen to. It wasn't supposed to be on the radio, it's not called radio music."

Chapter 15
Livin' In The Alley

Anthony "Miss Tony" Boston reigned as one of Baltimore club's most popular vocalists for a decade, but the last few years of his life were turbulent. He'd followed Frank Ski to 92Q and hosted *Off the Hook Radio* prior to it becoming Reggie Reg and later K-Swift's timeslot. But Boston was fired from the station in 1999, the same year that he suffered kidney failure, a consequence of years of heavy drinking and drug abuse.

Boston walked into a Baltimore church, Victory Center, in the late '90s with bags of dresses and high heels that he'd decided he'd no longer wear, and renounced his life as Miss Tony, working in the outreach ministry for the next few years. He didn't leave show business behind, but now went by Big Tony when performing in clubs or on records.

"Tony used to go to this church that my family went to," Tierre Brownlee says. "When his health was deteriorating, when he was real bad, my aunt took him in."

One of the last singles Boston released under the name Big Tony was far more vulnerable than the songs he'd made in the '90s. The "Livin' in the Alley" 12" was released in 2002 by High Rolla Records, with the A-side co-produced by Dukeyman and Boston. It's a song about Boston's rock bottom moment at an unspecified time in the past, when he'd been homeless: "It was a point in my life when I thought I had nowhere to go, and I thought the walls was closing down on me." But

Miss Tony's voice sounds hoarse and weak, perhaps due to his health issues, which enhances the sense of desperation in the song and hints that his troubles are far from over.

Even the neighborhood shoutouts at the end of "Livin' in the Alley" take on a poignant, pleading quality in the context of the song: "Park Heights, can you help me? Cherry Hill, can you help me?" House music lovers often praise the genre for its cathartic qualities, its big melodies and belting voices helping lead the listener to an ecstatic release of emotion. Baltimore club, with its rougher sound and more staccato vocals and bawdy lyrics, rarely offers that kind of conventional beauty or emotional release. But "Livin' in the Alley" broke new ground for Baltimore club as an unvarnished expression of one person's pain, even if it was still presented over an insistent dance beat.

The B-side of the single, "Storybook," featured Boston singing in a gentle falsetto about a fairy tale with a Baltimore twist: "Like in all the storybooks, the white knight came and took the little girl, alone in the world/ She might be from Cherry Hill, but she came to the Dox to get her life."

That same year, High Rolla released the sole full-length album by Boston, who was billed as "Big Tony aka Miss Tony." *Master of Ceremonies* mostly collected the majority of Boston's best-known singles and collaborations along with a few new tracks. It remains possibly the most essential Baltimore club album that is a collection of discrete songs rather than a continuous DJ mix, often uproarious and sometimes strangely touching. One later track, the Dukeyman-produced "Scream & Shout," has an overtly Christian message, essentially a praise song in the gospel tradition.

Anthony Boston died on April 11th, 2003, at Maryland General Hospital, at only 36 years old. Boston and Bernie

Rabinowitz, whose fatal car crash was three months earlier, were the first important figures in Baltimore club music that the scene mourned the passing of, but they wouldn't be the last.

The origin of one of Tony's best-known songs has come under dispute since his death. "Pull Ya Gunz Out," which was released on *Frank Ski's Club Trax – Volume 3* in 1993, was a quintessential Baltimore club shoutout song that came with its own dance, pointing finger guns in the air. The 1997 book *The Corner: A Year in the Life of an Inner-City Neighborhood,* by David Simon and Ed Burns, reporting from a block of West Baltimore over the course of 1993, even features a memorable vignette of teenagers dancing to "Pull Ya Gunz Out."

In 2008, Jimmy Jones told me that he'd been performing the "pull ya gunz out" chant at local parties before Miss Tony put it on record. "Let it be known, 'Pull Ya Gunz Out' started with Harford Road, where I'm from," Jones said. "Tony knew, too, before he passed away. I was always tellin' him, 'You knew you were wrong.' But it was always in fun, like he got out there first, the idea, he put it out there."

"I've heard Jimmy Jones say that before, Tony disagreed with that," says Diamond K. "Both of them were around in those early days, and I wasn't off the porch at that particular time, so I can't really say for sure. But I talked to both of them at different points in time [about it]."

These kinds of disputes aren't unexpected, given the context. The vocal hooks on Baltimore club records often originated as chants in the club that DJs, hosts, or audience members would start, repeat back to each other, or develop variations on. "A lot of those hooks, it would just be people in the crowd, just generally saying stuff. And we would get an idea, we'll go back the next day and make a track out of it," DJ Booman says. That sometimes exacerbated blurry issues of authorship in a scene where people were already using many of the same samples and frequently remixing each other's work.

Jimmy Jones passed away in 2021, and years later I heard yet another completely different origin story for "Pull Ya Gunz Out" from Tierre Brownlee. According to him, an acquaintance from Lexington Terrace who is also no longer living, Mowata Franklin (spelling unconfirmed), came up with the refrain one day while the go-go band Rare Essence's 1991 single "Lock It" was playing.

When Brownlee came up with his own variations on "Pull Ya Gunz Out," he delivered the chant over a "Think (About It)" breakbeat on DJ Tierre and DJ Paradise mixtapes. And after Miss Tony's version came out, they argued over the propriety of the hook. "I'll never forget this, Tony rides down Saratoga Street, he's in a jeep with a dude and a girl, and Tony's in the back," Brownlee remembers. "Tony jumped out the jeep, 'What's this I hear, you said I stole it from you?'"

Given that all three alleged authors of "Pull Ya Gunz Out" are now deceased, this particular debate will likely never be settled. The fact remains, however, that Miss Tony made the definitive recording of "Pull Ya Gunz Out," and it's a Baltimore club classic, part of his significant legacy within the genre.

"I think the thing that's interesting about Tony now is when Tony came out, to Baltimore's credit, honestly, he appeared to be extremely accepted and embraced and celebrated," says Baltimore journalist Lawrence Burney. "But I have a feeling that if Tony would've come out 15 or 20 years later, he might've actually blown up. I tell a lot of people, Miss Tony is kind of the Big Freedia before Big Freedia," he says, referencing the gender-bending New Orleans bounce icon who has appeared on hit songs by Beyonce and Drake.

Chapter 16
The New Dylan

In 2002, the Boston-based literary magazine *Post Road* published a piece entitled "Why Baltimore House Music Is The New Dylan" by Scott Seward, a wild-eyed New England record store proprietor and music critic with an infectious passion for a wide range of music. The sprawling and entertaining 4,000-word piece was a playfully provocative riff on one of the oldest tropes of rock criticism.

Bob Dylan rocketed to fame in the early '60s as a superstar of the folk music scene. When he abruptly retreated from the spotlight in 1966 after a mysterious motorcycle accident and began making inscrutable, divisive albums like 1970's *Self Portrait*, it felt as if he'd abdicated his throne as the de facto "voice of a generation." To some critics, it seemed there was a Dylan-shaped hole in the culture that needed to be filled.

Throughout the '70s, just about any intriguing new singer-songwriter was dubbed "the new Dylan" by the narrative-hungry music press. Future legends like Bruce Springsteen and John Prine bristled at Dylan comparisons and had to work harder to create their own unique legacies. Other new Dylans might have enjoyed or detested their time in the hype bubble before it inevitably popped and the media moved on to someone else.

By 1993, the concept had become such a familiar cliché that members of 10,000 Maniacs started a band called the

New Dylans. In 2002, dubbing anybody Dylan's successor in full seriousness was no longer a sexy pursuit, as music critics went in search of the next Kurt Cobain or 2Pac. Seward's celebration of Baltimore's gritty dance beats for *Post Road* was less a sincere *Rolling Stone*-style marketing pitch for the next big thing than a clever commentary on how tastemakers tended to ignore those kinds of bustling regional scenes, even if his enthusiasm unintentionally foreshadowed an explosion of media interest in Baltimore club in the following years.

Scott Seward's piece was dismantling the White-guy-with-a-guitar industrial complex, but also perhaps reinforcing it a little, by suggesting that Dylan's true next-generation heir was not another shaggy-haired folk singer writing long, complex protest songs. "If you say that a new Dylan has to be an adenoidal out-of-tune harmonica-muncher, then there is no room for argument. But if you say that the new Dylan is someone who is not afraid to reflect the world around them with biting vigor (and vigorous biting), to shock with the new and cut right through the bland in the hopes of making a new land for everyone, well then that could be anyone. Parliament/Funkadelic were the new Dylan and no one even cared. N.W.A. were the new Dylan, but they shocked virgin ears and people would not listen," he wrote.

Seward's suggestion, to take this logic one step further, was that the new Dylan was not necessarily one musician or group, but an abstract concept that could be personified by an entire city of primarily Black producers and DJs making profane, repetitive dance music. "If you search for pasty-faced folk-rockers you will find a mess of them. If you search for something that bewilders and scares you with its newness, you might just find the next Bob Dylan," he wrote. "And without a doubt, the Baltimore house music scene is one of the greatest new Dylans to appear in years." In so many words, Seward was putting his own spin on Brian Eno's idea of a collective "scenius" producing the kind of innovative work that critics often credit to a solitary genius figure.

Seward has mixed feelings about the piece today. "I'm not proud of all of it. It probably doesn't read well now," says Seward, who grew up in Connecticut with his brother Dan, frontman of the long-running noise/punk band Bunnybrains. Scott Seward lived in Philadelphia in the mid-'90s, running the short-lived record store Redrum, when one of the store's regulars, a DJ named Cosmo Baker, hipped him to club music. "Cosmo told me that when he played a Baltimore track during a DJ set, people would flip the fuck out. They were just immediate crow- pleasers."

Seward went to another Philly store that was known for selling Baltimore club, Funk-O-Mart on Market Street, and picked up the double LP *Unruly Tapemasters* compilation by DJ Sixth Sense, and quickly fell in love with what he heard. Incidentally, Sixth Sense was actually from Washington, D.C., and probably the first out-of-towner to make a credible Baltimore club mix for a Baltimore label. "It blew me away. I had no idea that people so relatively close to me were making their own unique party sounds," Seward says. "I was a big Miami bass fan back then. Baltimore club had that same ecstatic repetition and energy and humor of earlier bass music and also of that New York–style breakbeat house and freestyle. It basically had every element that I loved."

The next Baltimore records Seward bought were the DJ Class singles "Love Theme" and "Come Quick See," the latter of which was officially credited to 'DJ Class featuring 2 Black Guys Who Decided to Make Another Record Because the Rent Was Due, and This Is Better than Throwing a Rent

Party.' "To me, those two tracks are like some sort of platonic ideal for the genre," Seward says. His collection of Baltimore records quickly blossomed as he picked up anything he could track down, and Unruly became his new favorite label. "I couldn't get enough. I was high on the stuff. My love for Unruly was beginning to rival my love for Warlock or Pandisc or Sleeping Bag."

"In the early 2000s, I kept looking online for any info on Unruly or club music and I couldn't find anything, like nothing," Seward says. So the *Post Road* piece was, on some level, a response to the lack of existing journalism about Baltimore club, and it helped shine a light into the darkness and fill that void. "For the longest time it was still the only thing online you could read about this music, which seemed bizarre."

In 2003, Seward followed "New Dylan" with a shorter but more widely read piece, "Do Dew the Crabtown Clam," in the famed New York alt-weekly the *Village Voice*. "I am very proud of that piece," Seward says. "I worked hard on it and I really wanted to express what the music did to me, how it made me feel. And also map out a cobbled-together history of how club music came to be."

Seward started exchanging emails with Scottie B. and learning more about Baltimore club firsthand, and watched other writers eventually get wise to the music he'd been evangelizing about. "Little by little, the internet caught up."

Chapter 17
World Town

The internet gave rise to a confluence of several different cultural trends that helped make Baltimore club more widely fashionable in the early 2000s, including the increasing ease of downloading music, music blogs that distributed free MP3s, the novelty of bootleg remixes, and the introduction of technology that allowed DJs to mix a song into their set without owning it on vinyl. By the middle of the decade, "blog house" had become a thriving musical intersection where fans of dance music, hip hop, and indie rock met, with Baltimore club contributing a fair share of blog house's sonic DNA.

Since the '80s, hip hop labels had catered to DJs by releasing hit songs on 12" singles, usually offering instrumental and *a cappella* mixes of the song on the B-side of the record in order to "scratch" the vocal, stretch out the song, or otherwise personalize the track. This fostered the popularity of "blends," in which DJs would find multiple songs with the same tempo and play the vocal from one song over the beat from another song.

At a moment when rap/rock acts like Limp Bizkit and Kid Rock were extremely popular, but unfashionable with indie tastemakers, it was genre-clashing blends, rebranded as "mashups," that became a hipper, more critically celebrated way to bring hip hop and other genres together. Here were not just blends but juxtapositions of dramatically different genres or cultures, often with a humorous or irreverent subtext. The most popular mashups usually brought together Black and White artists you wouldn't expect to collaborate under normal circumstances, or indie and mainstream artists, high and low culture.

Freelance Hellraiser's "A Stroke of Genie-us," which combined pop star Christina Aguilera's vocals with a guitar-driven chug by acclaimed New York band the Strokes, became a trendsetting sensation on British radio in 2002. Danger Mouse's *The Grey Album*, editing vocals from Jay-Z's *The Black Album* over music from the Beatles' *White Album*, was one of the most acclaimed albums of 2004, despite the copyright holders of the original recordings serving cease-and-desist letters to the enterprising remixer.

It was in this mashup-crazy climate that DJ duos like Hollertronix and the Rub became popular in Philadelphia and New York with their omnivorous mixes of different genres. Hollertronix comprised Diplo and Low Budget, and the Rub comprised DJ Ayres and Cosmo Baker, the same guy who had first turned Scott Seward onto club music, a true Johnny Appleseed figure of Baltimore club's spread. Even in Baltimore, nights like the weekly dance party TaxLo, hosted by Cullen Stalin and Simon Phoenix, became a way for Baltimore's hipsters and college students to dance to club music without going to primarily Black clubs like the Paradox where the music had developed.

The New York Times named Hollertronix's *Never Scared* one of the ten best albums of 2003. But it wasn't an album in the conventional sense so much as a DJ mix, featuring the duo's own mashups of familiar pop music, new and old, such as Missy Elliott vocals over a song by the Clash, as well as mini-sets of different styles of dance beats from around the world. Jamaican dancehall, Indian bhangra, and Brazilian baile funk all figured into the mix, but one of the major selling points of *Never Scared* was that it was, for much of its audience, their first taste of Baltimore club music.

The 80-minute *Never Scared* featured, in its first half hour, an eight-minute suite of Baltimore club. The segment begins when the '80s electro rap classic "Supersonic" by J.J. Fad is transitioned into "Watch Out for the Big Girl" by Jimmy Jones. It ends with Rod Lee's "Feel Me" being mixed into Diplo's own attempt at a Baltimore club track, a remix of his song "Thingamajawn." The cover, a photo of smiling Black children holding water balloons, featured a sticker touting that the disc "includes the hit jawn 'thingamajawn' Baltimore version!" – "jawn" being something of a versatile all-purpose word in Philadelphia slang, reaffirming the mix's Philly origins even while touting its Baltimore sounds.

Without an itemized tracklist like a proper album, of course, it was impossible for the average listener to discern who made those songs, which often circulated as MP3s with "Baltimore club music" or even "Hollertronix" as the artist name instead of Jimmy Jones or Rod Lee. Someone who'd never heard a DMX vocal sample over a house track in Baltimore could reasonably assume that the juxtaposition was put together by Diplo or Low Budget themselves.

Wesley "Diplo" Pentz, a Florida native who grew up on Miami bass, had moved to Philadelphia to attend Temple University, where he fell in love with Baltimore club. In 2004, Diplo released an album of downtempo instrumental hip hop called *Florida* on the British dance label Big Dada, but he garnered far more critical attention for how he mixed and matched genres as a DJ.

Diplo's profile rose further with the 2004 mixtape *Piracy Funds Terrorism* by M.I.A., a vocalist born in Sri Lanka and based in London, who was quickly becoming one of the most critically acclaimed artists of the decade. "URAQT (Diplo Mix)" from that mixtape featured M.I.A.'s vocals over K.W. Griff's "You Big Dummy," a Baltimore club track that was built on a sample of Quincy Jones's theme song for the '70s sitcom *Sanford and Son*, as well as the humorous titular sample of dialogue from the show's star, Redd Foxx.

That remix proved so popular that it was featured on M.I.A.'s debut album for Interscope, 2005's *Arular*, instead of the unheard original mix of "URAQT" that presumably had no Baltimore club samples. The liner notes listed K.W. Griff as one of the track's four producers. But the only two credited songwriters are M.I.A. herself and Quincy Jones, raising age-old questions about whether the person who arranged and assembled a song's instrumental track should be considered one of its authors.

When hundreds of professional music critics voted in the *Village Voice*'s annual Pazz & Jop poll at the end of 2004, *Piracy Funds Terrorism* was ranked the 23rd-best album of the year. A year later, *Arular* placed at #2 on the same poll, right behind Kanye West. In all the ink spilled about M.I.A.'s subversive revolutionary politics and canny synthesis of an international potpourri of influences, nobody thought to crown M.I.A. the new Dylan. The original Dylan was in the midst of a late-career renaissance – he made it to #1 on Pazz & Jop in both 2001 and 2006 – and M.I.A. was praised for being the first M.I.A., a new archetype.

On the message board on Hollertronix's website, it became commonplace for producers from outside Baltimore to share their Baltimore club–inspired tracks, to the point that phrases like "white bmore" and "cluburbia" became the slanderous slang terms for inauthentic Baltimore club music. One forum moderator even devised a humorous autoreplace in the message board's code: if a user typed the word "corny" in a post, it would instead be published in the thread as "white bmore." The hipster crowd had become extremely self-conscious about its relationship with Baltimore club.

Unruly and other '90s Baltimore labels linked up with the out-of-towners who were now interested in the genre, and did what they could to capitalize on the renewed attention, selling their music through hip online retailers like Turntable Lab. Some locals were possessive about club music and suspicious of Diplo and his friends. But Scottie B. didn't see what was happening as all that different from what he and his friends had done a decade earlier, creating their own versions of styles that had originated in Chicago or New York.

"If people like something, they'll start emulating it. Just like Baltimore club emulated something that came before it. We took some other shit and we flipped it. People like to start the history when it benefits them." Scottie B. told *True Laurels* in 2014. "Music is like a kaleidoscope. It's the same shit inside of there and you can spin it a million times and get a million outcomes but the elements in there never change."

All this attention came at a time when Baltimore club's first-wave innovators had started to lose interest in the scene they created and let the younger generation take over local dancefloors. "We weren't even listening to it no more, really. It was just for the dancers and the kids, not like you goin' to an adult club and they playin' it," Scottie B. says. "You go out of town, it was older hipster crowds, they were in their 20s and 30s, or 40s."

"People don't realize that in the early '90s, 16-year-olds and 30-year-olds were listening to the same club music. When K-Swift and Blaqstarr took off, club music had become a younger music. Most people over 21, except maybe hipsters, didn't wanna hear it," Scottie B. told *True Laurels*. "Maybe not because of them individually, but it was the sound. It became a big dance contest."

Jason Urick, a Baltimore musician who recorded avant garde music for the Chicago-based indie rock label Thrill Jockey, invited DJ K-Swift to spin at Floristree, a DIY venue he ran in his downtown loft apartment, in 2005. Three hundred and fifty people attended the party, many of them White Baltimoreans who'd never heard club music in a club before.

"My manager booked it and we go there. I walk in and the building looks like the scariest thing I've ever seen in my life, graffiti everywhere, punk-rock kids, all this crazy weird stuff. Like, what kind of a party is this? I had no idea," K-Swift told *Spin*.

> "I thought it was a rock'n'roll party, but I get in there and everyone is dancing to Baltimore club. And when I walked in, they treated me like I was a queen, *for real*. 'Oh my gosh, she's here!' 'Can you sign an autograph?' Everyone was coming up to me to take pictures. I had some of my friends with me, and they started taking pictures with their camera phones because they couldn't believe these people were dancing to Baltimore club music. The best crowd I've ever DJ'd for in my life!"

DJ Technics sounded a note of skepticism in the same *Spin* piece about the buzz Baltimore club was now getting in a music industry that had ignored it for over a decade. "What we're doin', other people are interested in, but we're not interested in what they have to offer for it, because once again it will become their product and not ours," he said.

> "Major labels are only interested in making quick cash. They want you to modify, make changes, water it down, so the general public can understand it. But that's not what this is. It's rude, obnoxious, X-rated, and it's street, and just because it can be presented on a more commercial basis doesn't necessarily mean it should be."

In 2007, Blaqstarr was probably the most popular producer in Baltimore, and he increasingly became one of club music's foremost ambassadors to curious out-of-towners. Diplo signed Blaqstarr to his Mad Decent label and began releasing EPs of his tracks. When Diplo personally emailed me about posting Blaqstarr's new music on my blog *Government Names*, I was a little rude to him, and we engaged in a contentious exchange.

In one sense, I was probably trying to gatekeep a scene that wasn't mine to exclude anyone from. After all, I myself was just a White twentysomething music critic who'd gone to the K-Swift party at Floristree, even if it wasn't the first time I'd seen K-Swift spin. In another sense, I didn't resent Blaqstarr signing with a buzzy boutique label like Mad Decent so much as I dreamed of Blaqstarr signing to a major label to take his deeply original sound to the mainstream, like Timbaland. Those two situations may very well not have been mutually exclusive, but I was imagining a fork in the road for Baltimore club's future prospects.

M.I.A. came to Baltimore to work with Blaqstarr on her second album, *Kala*. Blaqstarr was only credited as co-producer on one song on the album, "The Turn," but made a more crucial contribution as a co-writer on another track, "World Town." Blaqstarr's local hit "Hands Up, Thumbs Down" had featured a young female voice, the producer's own sister, chanting the phrase "Hands up, thumbs down, represent that D-town" – meaning downtown, as in Downtown Baltimore, although some mistook the lyric as giving Baltimore a new nickname, "B-town." On "The Turn," M.I.A. modified the refrain to "Hands up, guns out, represent the world town," adding a component of violence to the lyric as well as nodding to the global melting pot aesthetic that had become her calling card.

Chapter 18
Dance My Pain Away

David Andler founded Morphius Records in 1993, initially releasing mostly music by local punk and indie rock bands. By the end of the decade, Morphius had expanded into a distributor for other labels, and had diversified into other genres. Stephen Janis of CLR, who by that point was well connected in Baltimore's club and hip hop scenes, was hired as chief operations officer of Morphius. A new arm of the company called Morphius Urban was launched, with Rod Lee and Baltimore hip hop legend Labtekwon as its marquee artists.

Vol. 5: The Official became Rod Lee's first mix CD distributed nationally by Morphius, which would eventually reissue Lee's earlier mix CDs, as well as *Operation: Playtime* by DJ Lil Jay, Lee's 14-year-old protégé. With more eyes on Baltimore club than ever before, *The Official* was covered by *Pitchfork*, *Spin*, and alt-weekly newspapers. "That was pretty exciting when we released the album," Janis says. "I think [Rod Lee]'s the main reason that Baltimore club became an international phenomenon."

Standing six feet and three inches tall and built like a linebacker, Rod Lee is physically imposing and speaks in blunt and often politically incorrect terms. By 2005, he was also towering over his peers in terms of commercial success, but he reached new heights in part due to a more tender and introspective song.

The Official featured what would quickly become one of the most famous Baltimore club songs of all time, "Dance My Pain Away." Singing in multi-tracked harmonies over a sparse track dominated by the "Think (About It)" break, Lee delivers melancholy lyrics from the perspective of a man who'd been laid off, hounded by repo men and fake friends, but found an escape on the dancefloor. If Big Tony's "Livin' in the Alley" was a breakthrough moment of emotional catharsis in Baltimore club, "Dance My Pain Away" was an even bigger milestone for a genre that had been considered – perhaps fairly, to an extent – to be a nonstop party with little self-reflection.

I was blown away by "Dance My Pain Away" the first time I heard it on 92Q. By that point, I'd been regularly posting Baltimore music on my MP3 blog *Government Names* for a year, but I hesitated to post the shorter excerpts of "Dance My Pain Away" that I'd found on the latest K-Swift and DJ Technics mixes, where it had appeared under a different title, "I Got Problems." So I was elated when *The Official* was released with the full "Dance My Pain Away" under its proper title, though it was still part of a mix, with other tracks bleeding into the beginning and end of the song.

"Dance My Pain Away" was inspired by Rod Lee's memories of how his mother, who'd died in 1996, would console herself with music. "My mother, she would get upset, she would just turn her music on," he says. "My brother was like, 'Yo, it sounds right.' It hit home, it's pain and you can dance to it. I said, 'Remember how mama used to…' and he said, 'Yeah.'"

The Baltimore-based arts journal *Link* published an issue in 2005 that spotlighted Morphius Records with a companion CD compilation featuring the label's artists. The issue featured Stephen Janis interviewing Labtekwon and Rod Lee, who opened up about his songwriting process more than he ever had before. "My music comes out of anger. Depressed anger that goes amongst everybody. You got people going to the club to have a drink cause they're mad at their females. You got guys going to club to get away from their bills. I just relate off everything," Lee told Janis. "If you could sit there and make someone dance after they got divorced, I know I'm good!"

At his peak as a hitmaker, though, Rod Lee also knew that "Dance My Pain Away" was a commercially savvy move, and uses a hilarious metaphor to express how deliberately he could tailor his music for maximum impact. "You remember when you were younger and you had a snowball battle? I'm the one that put the rocks in the snowball. So when I hit you, it's like, 'Ouch!' And I would laugh my ass off," he tells me with a chuckle.

Rod Lee had some tumult in his own life that may have given "Dance My Pain Away" some of its gravitas, but also might have hampered its success. In July 2005, just a few months after the song's release, Lee was convicted of second-degree assault, stemming from an incident that had happened the previous New Year's Eve. Lee gave interviews to *Spin* and the *Baltimore Sun* about his fast-rising career while serving six months in the Baltimore County Detention Center, and was ordered to attend anger management counseling. After serving his time, Lee continued making hits, and seemed determined to get his life on the right track. "My family is my top priority," he told the *Sun*. "I'm going to change the game."

"Dance My Pain Away" was massively popular in Baltimore, and became one of the rare club songs that made it into daytime rotation on 92Q, instead of being limited to airplay during DJ sets. It played a larger role in spreading the genre outside the city, though, and even in diversifying its following *in* the city.

Baltimore's indie rock scene had also blossomed in the mid-2000s, with several local bands signing to larger labels and building a national fanbase. One of those bands, the Merge Records duo Wye Oak, recorded a tender and melodic cover of "Dance My Pain Away" for *Baltimore Does Baltimore*, a 2009 compilation organized by the website *Splice Today*. "I'm honored," Lee says of the Wye Oak cover. In 2012, contestants on the Fox reality series "So You Think You Can Dance" did a choreographed routine to L.A. electronic group District 78's remix of the Wye Oak cover of "Dance My Pain Away."

"['Dance My Pain Away'] commented on the difficulties of life in Baltimore, in a way that I don't think any other [club] artist had done," says Janis. "Rod Lee was a genius enough to be able to take the elements of it and translate that into a song that was not only accessible to everyone but also did not depart at all from the Baltimore club feel, sound, and aesthetic."

Rod Lee's run with Morphius was mutually beneficial. "With Morphius, I still get checks to this day," he says. For his next mix CD, however, he teamed up with Unruly to release 2007's *The Producer*. "Dance My Pain Away" is largely a one-off in Lee's catalog, but one of the most popular songs on *The Producer* was something of a spiritual successor, celebrating the club as an escape from the unpleasant realities of workaday life. "Get your drink on/ Get your party on/ It could be worse, it could be worse," Lee chants on "Enjoy Yourself."

Chapter 19
The Wire

Throughout this period of burgeoning out-of-town attention around Baltimore club music, the city's top cultural export was *The Wire*, a panoramic crime drama about Baltimore's drug trade, law enforcement, and political establishment. The series, created by former *Baltimore Sun* journalist David Simon, aired on HBO for five seasons from 2002 to 2008.

Baltimore's rates of crime, murder, and heroin addiction had been well above the national average since the 1980s. And Simon's books and television series took an insightful, holistic view of the complex problems of American cities, and the futility of America's war on drugs. *The Wire* was also a highly entertaining show, full of comedy as well as tragedy, launching the careers of notable actors like Idris Elba and Michael K. Williams.

DJ K-Swift's Club Queen Entertainment was hired to market *The Wire* in Baltimore during its first season, well before it became one of the most critically acclaimed shows of its era. "We had the account for *The Wire*, and we had all the *Wire* hats, *Wire* things. They gave us a wrapped van," Porkchop remembers. "One day Swift woke up and said 'Wanna go to Atlantic City in the van?'"

The Wire was filmed on location, with many Baltimore natives in supporting roles, but in its early seasons, music was a weak spot in the show's sense of authentic local flavor. Most of the show's soundtrack was diegetic, meaning that the music the audience hears is also being heard by the characters within the show's reality. One particular Season 1 episode featured multiple songs by the New York conscious rapper and critical favorite Mos Def, suggesting a loose grasp on what kind of music you were most likely to hear coming out of Baltimore cars and bars in the early 2000s.

In later seasons of the show, however, music supervisor Blake Leyh – who was also responsible for the haunting instrumental music that plays over the end credits of each episode – got serious about including music by local acts in the show. "It wasn't until this season, Season 4, that I did the thing I should have done all along, which was to actually start using music from Baltimore," Leyh told *Baltimore City Paper* in 2006.

Prior to that, there actually was a little local music already in *The Wire*. In fact, Baltimore club music was featured in the show for the first time in the Season 3 episode "Hamsterdam." When drug dealer Bodie invited ex-con Cutty to a house party, the music at the function was "My Life Extra" by DJ Technics, a remix of the 2003 hit "My Life" by New Orleans rapper Juvenile.

That episode featured one of the more memorable plots in the show's run that wasn't based on anything that had actually happened in Baltimore in real life: a Baltimore PD scheme to functionally legalize drug dealing in one small part of city that was dubbed Hamsterdam. That storyline inspired a pair of Baltimore beatmakers, Darkroom Productions, to release a 2005 mixtape called *Hamsterdam – The Best of Baltimore*, with an all-star cast of local rappers including Comp, Ogun, and Tyree Colion on the duo's beats. Other rappers from the city were less subtle in trying to cash in on the attention *The Wire* brought to Baltimore. B. Rich of "Whoa Now" fame named his label the Wire Music Group, and released an album misleadingly titled *Hurry Up and Weight: The Wire Soundtrack*.

Upon hearing the *Hamsterdam* mixtape, Leyh was impressed and reached out to Darkroom Productions, putting several of the duo's tracks in Season 4 and Season 5. Baltimore club also returned to *The Wire* in the Season 4 episode "Unto Others," with Rod Lee's already iconic "Dance My Pain Away" in the background of a scene in which heroin addict Bubbles meets with his nephew Sherrod.

In January 2008, as *The Wire* was about to air its fifth and final season, the show finally got an official soundtrack album, in fact two of them. *The Wire: And All the Pieces Matter* intermingled Baltimore acts with the Tom Waits–penned theme song "Way Down In The Hole" and memorable needle drops from throughout the show's history by the Pogues and the Neville Brothers. A second album that was sold separately, *Beyond Hamsterdam: Baltimore Tracks from The Wire*, zeroed in on homegrown talent, ranging from the Rod Lee and Technics club tracks and Darkroom-produced hip hop to acclaimed jazz pianist Lafayette Gilchrist.

Both albums were released by Nonesuch Records, a Warner Music Group subsidiary best known for signing alternative rockers like Wilco and David Byrne. Given relatively little promotion, neither soundtrack album sold enough to appear on any *Billboard* charts. Of course, *The Wire* generally didn't receive mainstream accolades on par with the show's acclaim and cultural significance, having never won a single Emmy award, a fact that only reflects poorly on the Television Academy. But licensing those songs both enhanced the show's verisimilitude and brought an influx of money and attention to Baltimore's music scene – Rod Lee says he received ten thousand dollars for the use of "Dance My Pain Away."

One song featured in Season 4 of *The Wire* and on *Beyond Hamsterdam* that fused club music and hip hop was "That's Da Sound," a collaboration between the group Dirty Hartz and one of the city's most popular rappers of the era, Mullyman. "That's Da Sound" was co-produced by Debonair Samir and his new collaborator, Aaron "LaCrate" LaCanfora.

As hipsters in New York and other cultural enclaves became fascinated with Baltimore club, Aaron LaCrate was well positioned to act as a bridge between those worlds. After growing up in Highlandtown, spinning records in Baltimore as 'DJ Cool Aaron' under the tutelage of the legendary DJ Equalizer, LaCrate moved to Manhattan, where he founded the influential streetwear line Milkcrate. Returning to his roots, LaCrate launched a record label spinoff of his clothing line, Milkcrate Records, and began releasing Baltimore club tracks.

Debonair Samir was Aaron LaCrate's primary musical collaborator when Milkcrate Records began making serious moves in 2006. "I didn't even realize how big [club music] was until I did a party with Aaron in Miami in March," Samir told me that summer. "It was 90% Baltimore club music and they were losin' their minds. Everybody told me Bmore was big, I had to see it for myself. There were probably five thousand people in there, it was amazing to me. I was like, dang, Baltimore definitely got somethin'." With LaCrate's connections and Samir's experience making club tracks, the duo soon landed some big commissions, including official remixes for major stars like Madonna and Busta Rhymes.

The crime and poverty that plagued Baltimore, particularly during the years that Baltimore club music became the cathartic and celebratory sound of working-class Black Baltimore, had always been a subtext of out-of-town fascination with club music. Unfortunately, nobody played on this tension with lurid, sensationalistic tendencies quite like Milkcrate Records, which attempted to rebrand Baltimore club as "gutter music."

2007's *Wow, That's What I Call Gutter Music, Vol. 1* and 2009's *B-More Club Crack*, the latter of which was released nationally by the indie distribution giant Koch Records, featured some great tracks by Samir and his frequent collaborators. But Milkcrate adorned the CDs and its online promotions with photographs of boarded-up vacant Baltimore rowhouses, and drawings of crack vials next to a parody of the Baltimore Orioles logo with X's over its eyes. This was a grim reminder of the same urban blight and institutional neglect depicted in "The Wire," but with all the nuance stripped out and replaced with something tacky and almost nihilistic.

Scottie B., who'd known LaCrate for over a decade, seemed particularly displeased with LaCrate's style of selling Baltimore club to the world. Scottie took to wearing an anti-Milkcrate T-shirt with the words "Support Baltimore Club," and the Milkcrate logo surrounded by a red circle with a line through it. I interviewed both LaCrate and Scottie B. about their feud at the time, looking to cover the controversy for *City Paper*. Ultimately, though, I shelved an article about the Milkcrate/Unruly rift when it seemed to become too contentious to write about without possibly provoking legal threats from LaCrate. It also felt like a potentially unflattering story about internecine scene politics at a moment when Baltimore club was finally getting some overdue attention.

Unruly Records had slowed down its productivity around the turn of the millennium. Emboldened by renewed out-of-town interest in Baltimore club, as well as the signing of K-Swift and other popular younger DJs, though, Unruly revved back up into high gear in the mid-2000s. As the longest-running label with the largest back catalog, Unruly Records was well prepared to capitalize on the moment.

"The big thing we're gearing up for now is *Club Classics Vol. III*," Shawn Caesar told *Spin* in 2005. "That's gonna tell our story. That's going to have a ton of information with respect to where club music came from." *Unruly Club Classics Vol. III*, released in early 2006, was a double CD sequel to the series that had kicked off with two vinyl compilations in 1998. It was a mix of old and new, with one disc of unmixed tracks and one disc of a DJ mix by Scottie B., with music ranging from DJ Class and Karizma classics to new tracks by up-and-coming producers like Mike Mumbles and King Tutt.

King Tutt had begun making Baltimore club tracks in the late '90s as a teenager, and within a few years he'd begun impressing club veterans a decade his senior like Scottie B. and Rod Lee, whose Club Kingz label released Tutt's breakthrough "Shake My Ass." Tutt's ex-girlfriend had delivered the track's instantly memorable refrain: "I'ma shake my ass/ I'ma show my thong/ I'ma do what I want/ Ain't nothin' wrong."

"Scottie was like, 'Aw, you gettin' good now,'" Tutt remembered. "If Scottie likes your tracks, you good." Scottie, Tutt, and Shawn Caesar formed a group with the tongue-in-cheek name The Chavy Boys of London, DJing and making mixes as a trio. Scottie and Tutt also co-produced remixes that put a Baltimore club spin on tracks by other regional legends. The greats of Washington, D.C., go-go and Baltimore club finally collided in the form of Scottie and Tutt's club remix of Chuck Brown's comeback single "Chuck Baby." Scottie and Tutt also remixed the 2009 single "Faster Faster Pussycat (Let's Go!)" by Ultra Nate, the Baltimore house music diva whose Basement Boys–produced '90s hit "Free" was one of the city's greatest contributions to the dance music canon outside Baltimore club.

Chapter 20
410 Funk

K.W. Griff got his first chance to DJ on the radio in 1996 when he was asked to fill in for DJ Spen for one night on 92Q. That opportunity opened the door for Griff to become a mainstay of the station for over two decades. Other DJs, like Reggie Reg and K-Swift, may have been 92Q's most visible champions of club music in certain eras. But K.W. Griff was a constant through all those eras, helping to break countless Baltimore club songs and launch dozens of producers' careers.

"So many talented producers would provide me music, some of 'em I never met for like a year, two years. It was all email, they would just send me something. Some of 'em really didn't even think it was gonna be played," Griff says.

"I would play it right then and there, because I wanted to give everybody a chance. I was blessed to be on that platform and be able to utilize that to expose other producers. And also, it was kind of a win/win, it helped me, it helped the show because everybody looked forward to what was gonna be played on the club set on Fridays. And it also helped them, so they were producing more and creating more and sending more stuff and more people were hearing their names mentioned."

In most cities, it's a steep uphill battle to get heard on commercial radio stations, which stick to playlists full of big-name major-label acts. That was an issue for Baltimore rappers and R&B singers, few of whom got into 92Q rotation without a Rod Lee beat. For club music producers, however, nightly DJ mixes provided a chance for their latest tracks to be heard all over the city without going through the tedious process of getting approval from corporate radio execs.

"One thing I like about [Griff], he's not scared to give a person a chance," says Brandon "DJ B-Eazy" Harris, born in 1983, one of the many producers who got their radio breakthrough via K.W. Griff. "A lot of people are like, 'Aww, well, we not gonna play it.' They'll wait until somebody else plays it first."

In fact, B-Eazy's music got the attention of higher-ups at 92Q when the station's program director, Victor Starr, heard Griff play B-Eazy's club version of 50 Cent's 2007 single "Ayo Technology." Starr had the unorthodox idea of asking B-Eazy to expand his track into a full-scale remix, featuring 50 Cent's verses on a Baltimore club beat, and gave it prominent drivetime airplay over the original. Starr even sent it to 50 Cent's label, Interscope, in hopes of getting it released as an official remix.

Artaz Pierre Wilkins, born in 1991, was just nine years old when he began DJing. DJ Pierre (not to be confused with the Chicago house legend also known as DJ Pierre) was 15 when he started sending music to K.W. Griff. "I was testing, I just sent him two tracks, to see if he got 'em and played 'em. I listened to the radio that night, I was like, 'Oh, alright, that really was his email.' He played both of 'em, too. I was so happy, that was the first time I heard my tracks on the radio." Baltimore club music producers born in the '80s had just gotten a foot in the door a few years earlier, and now a producer born in the '90s was in the mix as well.

"When you love music and you're surrounded by great people, that time just goes by. You do it every week and you don't even think anything of it. Next thing you know, 21 years gone by," Griff told the *Baltimore Sun* in 2017, when he stepped away from his longtime post doing the 9 o'clock mix.

The Doo Dew Kidz sometimes felt neglected by the new wave of national attention lavished on Baltimore club music. DJ Booman wrote an irritable post on his MySpace page in 2006:

"If I read another blog, see another TV program, or see another magazine mention the history of the club scene and not mention the trailblazers like myself, KW Griff, Jimmy Jones, Technics, 2 Whyte Kydz, DJ Class, Karizma, Patrick, Diamond K, Chase, Kenny B, Foe, Tapp, Tony, Boobie, Rod Braxton and the countless others that contributed to the most influential time in the music, there's going to be a problem!"

Within a couple of months of that post, however, Booman landed some notable industry placements, producing official remixes of the Jim Jones hit "We Fly High" and the Sean "Diddy" Combs track "Get Off." A decade after being served a cease-and-desist letter for sampling SWV, Booman was finally getting paid by big labels to make Baltimore club remixes.

By the mid-2000s, Booman was deeply embedded in Baltimore's blossoming new-school hip hop scene, as the DJ for live performances by rising stars like Mullyman, D.O.G., and Golden Seal, and spinning at Team Fifty events at Five Seasons. But he also saw the way club music was spreading like wildfire outside Baltimore like never before, and began booking gigs in New York City, where he was asked to spin

Baltimore club. "New York used to never give club music love," he says. "It's pretty cool."

If there was anyone who had even deeper roots in Baltimore hip hop than DJ Booman, it was Labtekwon, a prolific and deeply original rapper whose catalog of albums stretched all the way back to 1988. "He was probably the first guy that I know that ever wanted to rap on a club beat way back in the early '90s. But a lot of people back then just laughed at it," Booman said.

Labtekwon's music had remained grounded in jazzy loops and midtempo grooves, but by the mid-2000s he had begun to gesture more often towards club music as part of his hometown's cultural DNA. "It ain't booty shake, we call our music club," he rapped on "Windows," from 2005's *The Ghetto Dai Lai Llama: African Rhythm American Blues*. On "Dr. Strangelove" from the 2006 follow-up *Avant God*, he rapped over Baltimore club's most iconic breakbeat, "Think (About It)," albeit at a slower tempo.

Later that year, Labtekwon took a full dive into the genre for the first time, forming a new group called 410 Pharaohs with Booman and Jones. They were the most qualified possible team to fuse Baltimore club and hip hop together, with Booman's beats, Lab's rhymes, and Jones's chants and hooks. But it was actually the culmination of a long friendship and creative journey for the three of them.

"What we're gonna show them with Labtek is that you can be a straight MC, you can rap about what you wanna rap about, you don't have to rap about shakin' ass," Booman said. That's not to say that there was no ass shakin' on 410 Pharaohs' songs. Their debut single, "Sex Machine," was a rare instance of a Labtekwon track that received airplay on 92Q.

Strictly Rhythm, the pioneering dance label that released many house tracks that had influenced early Baltimore club, was relaunched in 2007 after a few years of inactivity, and soon signed 410 Pharoahs. The group also lined up sponsorship from Toyota Scion, an auto brand marketed to millennials that often aligned itself with underground hip hop acts, for a series of concerts in March 2007.

As with the Doo Dew Kidz, 410 Pharaohs' songs often started with Jimmy Jones. "I'd say out of the whole album, I did the majority of comin' up with the concepts, except for like two [songs]. I'd come up with the hook and the theme of the song, and they'd feed off that, Lab would feed off that," Jones said.

The album *410 Funk*, released in 2008, featured "Big Girls," a new version of Jones's signature song "Watch Out for the Big Girls," as well as revisiting "Shout" on the title track. The album wasn't entirely a trip down memory lane, however, offering the new blueprint for lyrical rap over club beats that Booman had promised. "No More Sorrow" was the album's masterpiece, the rare song that could unlock Baltimore club's emotional potential as brilliantly as Rod Lee's "Dance My Pain Away."

"That 410 Pharaohs album, that could've been, like, our *It Takes a Nation of Millions to Hold Us Back*," says DJ Kool Breez. "It really could've been big. That's why my hat's off to Booman."

410 Pharaohs proved to be short-lived, with Lab walking away from the project before a second album could be made. But Booman and Jones kept it moving, returning to releasing conventional club music tracks like 2009's "Slick Flair," sampling wrestler Ric Flair.

Labels outside Baltimore were also taking an interest in

reissuing club music's classics. I was contacted by Crosstalk, a Chicago-based dance music distributor that sold vinyl in America, Japan, and Europe. What little Baltimore club they had in stock was selling well, and they were looking to make more available. I posted a notice on my blog, *Government Names*, that Crosstalk was eager to connect with Baltimore club producers, and the label was soon contacted by DJ Technics, Rod Lee, and Diamond K, among others.

The first record in Crosstalk's series, *Baltimore Club Classics Vol. 1*, was released in April 2008, featuring six of Dukeyman's best tracks. The first time I met Dukeyman, in 2006, he'd already started to feel like Baltimore club was part of the past. "To me, right now, club music is dead, done. Done and dead. None of the stuff that people puttin' out now will ever be classics," he said. "These songs now, they go in rotation for like a week."

By 2008, when I talked to Dukeyman about his Crosstalk release, he had pretty much ceased making new club tracks, still feeling disconnected from the younger generation that was now running the scene. "Me makin' [tracks] is not the problem, I'm not just gonna sit here makin' 'em, and try to chase down these DJs that are gonna play my song," he told me at the time. "I'm from the old school, there's a whole bunch of new cats."

Chapter 21
The Spongebob

By the mid-2000s, Baltimore club music was getting faster (sometimes pushing above 130 BPM), the fanbase was getting younger, and the dancing was becoming more athletic and choreographed. Teenagers would come up with moves they could do together in unison, or taking turns in the spotlight on the dancefloor, like the Crazy Leg or the Slide, which was set to Blaqstarr's "Slyde." "I used to enjoy watching the kids dance to it, doing the Crazy Leg or whatever was goin' on at the time, because the tempo was so up," says Wayne Davis.

DJ Tigga was dancing in the clubs for years before he made the transition to the DJ booth and then to producing. And because he had friends in the local dance crews who'd create routines to particular songs, he'd often get requests to make Baltimore club versions of popular rap and R&B hits. "Right now, the remix thing is what everybody likes. Some guys will come to me and they're like, 'Can you make this into a club song so we can dance to it?' And that's how the remix comes about, so they can perform with it," he told me in 2007, when his club versions of Rich Boy's "Throw Some D's" and Omarion's "Ice Box" were locally popular.

One of the most famous dances of the era was the Spongebob, named after the massively popular Nickelodeon cartoon character Spongebob Squarepants. DJ and producer John "Jonny Blaze" Grant, a devoted father of seven children, got the idea for the track that started the craze from one of his kids. "I used to lay there with my daughter and son and watch Nickelodeon. They'd be like, 'Man, that's a nice song, what you think of that?'"

Jonny Blaze collaborated with Mike Mumbles on a 12" called *Kiddie Disco Time* that sampled a wide variety of cartoon theme songs, including *Dora the Explorer*, *Fairly Odd Parents*, and, of course, *Spongebob Squarepants*. "I gotta give my daughter credit for the Spongebob, because I would never have thought of it," he says.

Baltimore club music has often ventured into sampling cartoons, sometimes humorously juxtaposed with more explicit content – like, say, DJ Tigga's popular club remix of Three 6 Mafia's "Slob on My Knob" that features a cameo by Stewie, the talking baby from the animated sitcom *Family Guy*. Jonny Blaze's cartoon cuts, by contrast, are generally safe for all ages.

Perhaps it was all that quality time with his kids that also that made Jonny Blaze adept at DJing for any kind of audience. "I like playing for a younger crowd, because I got a lot of energy. Sometimes when I'm playin' for an older crowd, I can't bring that energy out. But when I play for a young crowd, I can give them a show. All that energy, I just bring it out, then go home and go to sleep," he says. "There's a lot of DJs out there that's sayin' they're playing Baltimore club music, but they're not. From what I hear, they're playing their interpretation of Baltimore club music. I'm givin' it to 'em gritty, just straight hard 808."

After working on tracks with DJ Patrick in the late '90s, Jonny Blaze struck out on his own in the early 2000s, downloading a DAW called Reason at the recommendation of a Guitar Center employee. "My first track on Reason was

'Spongebob' and I gave it to Griff. [K-Swift] loved it too, gave it to her and the rest is history, started puttin' out record after record after record."

Jonny Blaze released a number of lasting tracks on his label Blaze One Records, including "Run Bitch Run" and "Can You Fuck Like You Dance," but it was the cartoon-sampling track that had the biggest legacy, inspiring one of the most iconic dance moves in Baltimore club history. The Spongebob is relatively simple, but difficult to do well: the dancer kicks one leg out while shifting their weight to the other leg, then alternates, as quickly as possible in time to the music. The move quickly became popular to pair with other tracks, but it kept the name that tied it to its original inspiration.

Jonny Blaze remembers the night he walked into the Paradox and saw a crowd doing the Spongebob to his track for the first time. "I think [Supa DJ Big L] was playin' it, and I seen this guy rockin' off to it. And I'm lookin' at him like 'What the hell is he doin'?' So my buddy was like, 'That's the Spongebob.'" Jonny Blaze laughs off the idea of ever doing the dance himself. "I'm a big guy, so you wouldn't see me doin' that. After the first couple moves I'd get a heart attack." Eventually, though, Jonny Blaze saw how effective it was to have a famous dance move associated with a track, even releasing a music video for his 2009 track "My Ice Cream" with DJ Patrick and D'Asar, featuring instructions for an accompanying dance step.

At some point, the Spongebob escaped Baltimore – there's even a "Spongebob Shuffle Tutorial" on TikTok, breaking down the moves in slow motion: "1. Kick, 2. Hop in center, 3. Repeat." There's nothing about the way the creator dances or dresses, or the EDM track in the background of the TikTok, that suggests anybody involved in the video has ever stepped foot in Baltimore or even heard club music. In recent years,

Jonny Blaze himself has become active on TikTok – he still samples cartoons, like the Disney film *Encanto* or the '80s series "Voltron," but can now create videos that sync his club tracks up to the animation from the source material.

Jonny Blaze's partner in Blaze One Records, DJ Ron Rico, also found success in sampling children's television. "The biggest thing, as far as the club music, was the cartoons," Ron Rico says. "I started doin' things with cartoons. A lot of old alphabetical records I had, old stuff I got when I was a kid, I started experimentin' with that." One of Ron Rico's most popular tracks, "Miss A," sampled the '70s PBS educational series *The Letter People*.

Jonny Blaze's name was inspired by Johnny Blaze, the Marvel Comics antihero better known as Ghost Rider, which became a popular nickname for a number of rappers and producers, including Wu-Tang Clan's Method Man. In fact, the first time I met a hip hop producer named Johnny Blaze, at a Baltimore "beat battle" tournament, I mistakenly thought he was the Baltimore club producer, eventually meeting Grant himself a couple of years later. "Man, it's like hundreds of 'em. They hit me up on MySpace, 'How long have you had your name?'" he says. "I had it since like '88. I got a lot of 'em beat, a whole lot of 'em."

While Marvel's Johnny Blaze made a pact with Satan, however, Baltimore club's Jonny Blaze is a devout Christian. And perhaps making some of Baltimore club's most family-friendly hits also made Jonny Blaze an ideal candidate to fuse club with praise music.

Gospel house has existed for decades, but it split off from early house music in an almost perfectly opposite direction from Baltimore club music, emphasizing slick piano-heavy production and big vocal harmonies, and of course more wholesomely uplifting lyrics. So Jonny Blaze's decision to combine gospel and Baltimore club on his 2012 album *The Transition* was a bold, novel idea.

The album featured original songs like "Here We Go," the single that caught the attention of the gospel label Tate Music Group, who made it Blaze's first nationally distributed record. The album also reworked older club tracks with religious themes: "Jesus is the Way" is based on "Priceless" by DJ Mook and Nafoe, and "Pray My Pain Away" is based on "Dance My Pain Away," although Rod Lee didn't appreciate the homage. "He didn't like it. I felt bad," Blaze says. Blaze made the album at a difficult time in his life, when his wife left him and took the kids with her. "God got me through, because a lot of that pain went into my music, so I had an outlet."

Chapter 22
Next Level

By the mid-2000s, DJ K-Swift was arguably the most popular radio personality in Baltimore, and had started to making the jump to national television. In 2004, she appeared as the in-house DJ on an episode of BET's *Rap City: The Bassment*. When MTV News came to Baltimore in 2006 to cover the club scene, K-Swift was the hometown representative who took cameras to the Paradox, spotlighting songs by Rod Lee and Blaqstarr. The three-minute segment gave a brief summary of club music's history, with MTV correspondent Sway Calloway nodding to the genre's roots and early breakthroughs like "Doo Doo Brown."

In 2005, K-Swift started a new venture, Next Level Productions, which seemed aimed at leveraging her growing fame and tastemaking clout into real music industry power. Black teen culture was becoming big business in the mid-2000s at the height of the Scream Tour and BET's request countdown show *106 & Park*, with teen idols like Bow Wow, Omarion, Chris Brown, and Ciara dominating mainstream radio. 92Q's airwaves began filling with teen rappers managed by Next Level, rapping over tracks by Baltimore club producers, positioned for maximum commercial potential.

The first Next Level artist was Young Leek, a 15-year-old rapper from New Jersey whose debut single set Baltimore on fire. Blaqstarr had kept a track in his back pocket for months:

an infectious loop of his voice saying "shake it and jiggle it" over bouncing tom-toms, a 107 BPM groove that was slower than his Baltimore club material.

"I'd play it at parties here and there, mix it with a capellas, and then a group of girls would make a dance to it," Blaqstarr remembers. "Then I started DJin' at Hammerjacks through Swift, she heard the track. She was like, 'Ooh, Blaq, I gotta get that. I got the right artist for it and everything. Just trust me on this, Blaq, I'll set this up.' So she put it all together like that, introduced me to Leek."

K-Swift put "Jiggle It" into heavy rotation on 92Q and made Young Leek into a celebrity in Baltimore. Leek worked on a follow-up track with Stay Gettin' Productions, a pair of beatmakers who had worked their way up from producing Baltimore artists like Tim Trees to major label stars like Cam'ron. Like K-Swift, Stay Gettin's Mike Miller and Lawrence Simpson saw Leek's potential to be the next Bow Wow, and had dollar signs in their eyes. "We did the song, went outside to talk for like 20 minutes, and were like, 'Can you imagine what we could do with this kid?" remembers Miller.

Stay Gettin' flexed their industry connections and brought Plain Pat – a producer and Kanye West associate who was an A&R man at Def Jam at the time – down to Baltimore to see Leek perform in October 2005. K-Swift held a birthday party event at Hammerjacks the night after she turned 27, and a camera crew was on hand to shoot a music video for "Jiggle It." The video was never released, but Def Jam was interested, and after a showcase in New York for label chairman L.A. Reid, Young Leek became a Stay Gettin' Entertainment/ Def Jam artist. The only real difference between the original local release of "Jiggle It" and the major-label version was that Leek re-recorded his ad libs on the song's intro, replacing Blaqstarr's name with a shout out to Def Jam.

Young Leek was fast-tracked to release his Def Jam album *Somethin' To Prove* in 2006, but "Jiggle It" never quite took off nationally, and the album was shelved. Later that year, however, Leek was namechecked in a Season 4 episode of HBO's *The Wire*. When Marlo Stanfield's drug running business faced the threat of New York dealers coming down to Baltimore and working on his territory, Stanfield's enforcers Chris (Gbenga Akinnagbe) and Snoop (Felicia Pearson) were charged with sniffing out the out-of-town interlopers. Chris suggested that Snoop "ask a Baltimore question, like… who Young Leek be?" Several Baltimore musicians may have had their music featured in *The Wire*, and rapper Skarr Akbar had a brief speaking role, but Young Leek getting his name dropped in a classic scene on the show gave him a greater level of Baltimore immortality, even if he wasn't actually from Baltimore

Blaqstarr's song "Slyde" was remixed by the Next Level rapper Tae-Eazy, who shot a video for the track at Club Choices. Another Next Level rapper, A-Maz-On, signed to Interscope off the strength of a couple of Say Wut–produced tracks. Blaqstarr's "Hands Up, Thumbs Down," was remixed by the Next Level group Deuce Tre Deuce before it inspired M.I.A.'s "World Town."

"Hands Up, Thumbs Down" had another offspring in DJ Manny's hit "Down the Hill," which sampled the sound of Blaqstarr's sister saying the phrase "Hey down the hill." In fact, Manny's track was a Frankenstein comprising pieces of several Baltimore classics, including K-Life's "Let's Get High" and Debonair Samir's "Samir's Theme." "I kinda revamped the whole thing and mixed it up with a few other samples, and came up with the track," DJ Manny explains. "So I always tell everybody, [Blaqstarr] was the first one to do it, I give him that credit." Rod Lee got in on the trend with his teen collaborator, DJ Lil Jay, on the song "What Chew Know About Down the Hill."

Baltimore is an extremely hilly city with several areas and neighborhoods named after hills: Cherry Hill, Druid Hill, Federal Hill, Butchers Hill, Bolton Hill, Reservoir Hill, Seton Hill, Marble Hill, even Shipley Hill. So is there a specific meaning to "Down the Hill"? Even DJ Manny acknowledges that opinions differ in the city. "Anything below North Avenue is considered down the hill" – the street that Odell's once stood on is, indeed, uphill from downtown and the waterfront. Manny adds with a shrug, "Some people say they down the hil, and they might be on 20th Street. It's so many hills, Greenmount is nothing but a hill."

One excellent track fusing hip hop and club music that was lost in the shuffle was 2004's "Face Down," which Blaqstarr produced for Bossman's N.E.K. crew shortly before the Rod Lee–produced "Oh" made him a local star. When Bossman signed to Virgin Records in 2005 and released a mixtape, *This Is a Warning*, with New York radio personality DJ Envy, "Face Down" was included, as Bossman used the song to explain the Baltimore club sound to Envy in an interlude. But the song was never promoted by Virgin or considered for Bossman's major-label debut, even as its producer was becoming a brand name both locally and nationally.

Soon after K-Swift built up her roster of Next Level artists, Blaqstarr began working with his own teen rapper protégé, Ryeisha "Rye Rye" Berrain. Blaqstarr was friends with Rye Rye's older sister when he took note of the Dr. Samuel L. Banks High School student's musical talent. "He was on the phone with her one time, and he just randomly asked her did I know how to rap," Rye Rye told me. In fact, she did rap, and impressed him on the spot with her rhymes. "Earlier that day I was writing a song, and it inspired me to make a whole track. So I wrote the song out, and then I called his voicemail and I rapped the song on his answering machine."

Rye Rye says she'd looked up to K-Swift as a role model in the scene, but sadly didn't get to know her, despite their mutual friend. "I feel like we just never got the chance to ever cross paths because, y'know, she had her thing going on. She had a whole team of guy artists, and Blaqstarr just had me."

K-Swift also sometimes commissioned tracks from producers, often to make anthems to represent her clique, a group of girls who called themselves the Ryders. From 2003 to 2005, there were several from Rod Lee and his Harm Squad label, including Lee's "K-Swift Get Freaky" and "Ridaz," and a track from the singer Urban Legend that praised K-Swift as "the hottest female DJ in Baltimore today."

A track Blaqstarr dropped in early 2006 was bigger than every previous song namechecking K-Swift combined. "One day we was at Hammerjacks, she was like, 'Blaq, why don't you try to make a track for Ryders for me," the producer remembers. "So I went home and put my herbs and spices in the pot." The track, featuring strobing synth arpeggios and a massive vocal hook, was called "Ryda Gyrl," and it was an instant phenomenon. I can think of few local songs, club music or otherwise, that had the same kind of impact – I remember walking down Broadway in Fells Point and hearing a woman singing, "My ryda, my ryda, my ryda gyrl." On the original version of the song with verses by Blaqstarr, the producer raps a few flirtatious lines about K-Swift before demurring that their relationship is "strictly business."

D.O.G., a Baltimore rapper who was a little older than the Next Level kids and patterned himself after New York street rappers like the Diplomats, heard potential in the song. His manager Poppa Guac reached out to K-Swift about making a rap remix of "Ryda Gyrl." "They contacted Swift, and was like, 'Yo, we wanna buy that track from that dude,'" says Blaqstarr. "So she was like, 'You wanna get with 'em, see how far it go?'" And it went far, spreading through the mid-Atlantic region faster than any other Baltimore track of the era, even "Jiggle It." D.O.G's version was so popular that it got him signed to Universal Records, who added Atlanta rap star Yung Joc to the song. There was even a Ryda Gyrl clothing line, with black and white baby tees adorning the song's female fans all over the city.

Martin O'Malley was mayor of Baltimore from 1999 to 2007, and one of the more ambitious initiatives of his two terms in office was the Believe campaign, launched in 2002. The logo, bearing the word "Believe," was plastered all over the city, on public buildings as well as on trash cans, a slogan linked to city government initiatives aimed at reducing rates of crime and drug use in Baltimore and reversing the city's economic decline.

Richard Burton, known to *The Wire* fans for playing Shamrock, a member of the Barksdale crew, became chief field coordinator of the Believe campaign. Burton masterminded the Baltimore Believe Tour, a recurring event for several summers that combined live entertainment with booths offering social services from city departments. The BelieveMobile, a tractor trailer with a massive 28-foot "BELIEVE" logo on the side, would convert into a flatbed stage for concerts outside public schools or at intersections like Edmondson and Carey in West Baltimore.

Occasional Believe Tour events featured R&B legacy acts like the Stylistics and Harold Melvin's Blue Notes, but the entertainment was primarily curated by 92Q. The station's on-air personalities would help Burton host the proceedings, and the best-known Baltimore rappers, from Bossman to Tim Trees, would perform clean versions of their hits.

There was a little tension in Baltimore street rappers performing at an event sponsored by the Baltimore Police Department. *Stop Fuckin' Snitchin'*, an underground DVD that came out of the Baltimore hip hop scene, made national headlines for threateningly discouraging witnesses and victims of crime from complying with police investigations. D.O.G., who sneeringly referred to the Baltimore Believe Tour as "the Baltimore Police Tour" on a 2005 mixtape track, had a change of heart and became one of the event's headline performers in 2006. "I didn't really understand it," he says. "When they told me it was for the kids and stuff like that, I said, 'OK, that's what I want to do. That's who I want to reach.'"

One Believe Tour stop I saw at Dunbar High School in the summer of 2006 felt like a showcase of K-Swift's ability to launch local stars. K-Swift would spin club music for dancing teens, and Young Leek, D.O.G., Cooli Hi, and Tay-Eazy took turns performing their Blaqstarr-produced hits, with Blaqstarr sometimes appearing onstage with them.

Baltimore is known all over the world for its Chesapeake Bay crabs. But when someone in Baltimore says the phrase "crabs in a barrel," they might not be talking about having steamed crabs with Old Bay for dinner. When a batch of live crabs is gathered in a bucket or a barrel, and the crab closest to the top tries to climb out, you might actually see one of the other crabs grab them with a claw to pull them back down. This is often seen as a metaphor for human nature, especially in

Baltimore: one person starts to thrive, make it out of poverty and get a better life for themselves, and people from their own hometown start trying to drag them down.

While it would be accurate to say that K-Swift was wildly popular in Baltimore during her lifetime, she was not without detractors, crabs in a barrel nipping at her heels. An anonymous letter addressed "To All Government, Public, And Media Officials," was widely circulated through the Baltimore music scene as an email forward in May 2007. The letter demanded an "immediate investigation" into payola and corruption at 92Q, alleging that "the only local artists/labels that have consistently received radio play are those that are produced by K-Swift and other K-Swift/92Q affiliated DJs, mainly Rod Lee."

This was a sensationalized exaggeration, but there was a grain of truth there: much of the local music that thrived on 92Q came through DJs who worked for the station, and through K-Swift's record pool. It wasn't entirely different from the system that New York hip hop had thrived on, with radio personalities like DJ Kay Slay and Funkmaster Flex hyping records by the same artists who appeared on their albums and mixtapes. Open conflicts of interest like this had seemingly been accepted as business as usual, because these were popular artists and DJs who were at the forefront of the culture, ethics be damned.

K-Swift never directly responded to the anonymous letter, but she made her feelings known with the title of the July 2007 mix CD *Jumpoff Vol. 11: Not Guilty*, which opened with a courtroom skit in which she denied any wrongdoing without addressing any specific allegations. In May 2008, I posted about another K-Swift mixtape on my blog, and an anonymous commenter simply responded, "Fuck K-Payola."

K-Swift's place at 92Q was secure, but Rod Lee's

relationship with the station came under scrutiny. The station was in an impossible situation: it was the world's greatest broadcasting platform for an entire homegrown genre, but the only way to credibly present Baltimore club music was by employing the same DJs who made the music and ran the labels that released it.

Rod Lee, who had been hired by program director Dion Summers in 2000, played music by all his Baltimore club contemporaries, but he also inevitably played his own music. The next program director the station hired, Victor Starr, took a closer look at Lee's arrangement with 92Q after the circulation of the letter. "Victor pulled up my contract and pulled me in the office, was like, 'I've never seen this before, I've never seen a DJ get hired to play his own music.'"

Lee, who was only interested in spinning music on the air, was also asked to do van runs, broadcasting from remote locations around the city while promoting the station. That was ultimately the sticking point that made him walk away from 92Q in 2008, although his music would remain ubiquitous on its airwaves.

"He pushed me in a corner, and it started irritatin' me. And I was like, 'Y'know what? I'm gone. I can't do this shit,' and I left," Lee says. "Swift was there, she was in the hallway, I gave her my badge, and she was standin' there cryin'. She was like, 'Don't go, don't go, we'll just talk to 'em.' And I just looked at Swift, like, 'You know how I get down, I'm not doin' this.'" An era was coming to an end in 2008, but in a much more profound way than anyone realized in that moment.

Chapter 23
The Club Queen

The third weekend of July 2008 was a great time to be in Baltimore, or at least it felt like one until Monday morning. The first Artscape festival was held in 1982, the year I was born, and every summer for most of my life, Artscape would take over a large area in the center of Baltimore for what often seems to be the hottest weekend of the year, a sprawling mass of performance stages and street vendors across Mount Vernon and surrounding neighborhoods. The Main Stage headliners were often R&B acts with wide appeal – in 2008, it was Roberta Flack, Ne-Yo, and newly reunited hometown heroes Dru Hill. But the most exciting thing about that year's festival was that it was the first time it felt like Baltimore club music was being properly celebrated at Artscape.

On Friday, I left my Mount Vernon office job at the end of the workday and walked a few blocks up to the festival grounds. I spent hours at the DJ Culture Stage that weekend, seeing Blaqstarr spin a relentless set of his hits on Friday night, and then returning for DJ K-Swift the Club Queen's Saturday afternoon set. At Artscape, K-Swift turned the audience into a vibrating mass of bodies with a mix heavy on Say Wut and Rod Lee club tracks. Swift yelled, "If you ready to shake off, make some noise!" as she transitioned from DJ Class's "Tear Da Club Up" to Blaqstarr's "Hands Up, Thumbs Down," moving from older tracks for the "25 and over crew" to the more recent hits she'd helped popularize.

K-Swift did reach a bit outside the borders of Baltimore to play one of her favorite recent songs: M.I.A.'s "Boyz." She let longtime friend and veteran party host Buck Jones handle microphone duties so she could focus on the mix. Towards the end of her set, however, K-Swift got on the mic and spoke hopefully about bringing Baltimore club to international audiences.

That Monday morning, July 21st, I woke up to get ready for work and saw that my phone had been filling up with text messages for hours. Something bad had happened, but it took a few minutes to piece together exactly what. "R.I.P." comments were all over K-Swift's MySpace page. Fred Keene, editor of the local hip hop publication *Mic Life Magazine,* sent me the tip that I posted on my blog at 7:44am before I went to work: "Just heard from a reliable source that K-Swift just died at Good Samaritan Hospital from a head injury sustained from a swimming pool."

Khia "K-Swift" Edgerton died three months shy of her 30th birthday, in the prime of her career, and on the cusp of bigger things. Later, it was revealed that she was in the midst of booking her first overseas shows, and that her label, Unruly Records, had just inked a deal with Koch Records the weekend of Artscape. The massive independent distributor had recently turned another regional radio personality and disc jockey, Miami's DJ Khaled, into a household name, and had its eye on K-Swift as Unruly's breakout star. "It was sad that it happened the same day," says Shawn Caesar. "It was unreal."

There was a wake on the Thursday after K-Swift's death, a viewing on Friday, and then the funeral on Saturday. That week, tribute songs started pouring in. Diamond K and the Baltimore-influenced New Jersey producer DJ Tameil collaborated on "The Ones We Lost," and Baltimore rapper Skarr Akbar released "The Eulogy (My Own Way)." Bossman recorded "I Wonder" with Washington, D.C. R&B star Raheem DeVaughn, with a music video featuring footage of K-Swift's funeral procession that showed an entire city in mourning.

The weekend after K-Swift's death, Blaqstarr performed at the Rock The Bells Tour, dedicating his set to her. National media outlets including *Vibe* and *XXL* published obituaries. DJ Drama, perhaps the most famous hip hop DJ in America at the time, shouted, "Rest in peace, K-Swift," on *Dedication 3*, the highly anticipated mixtape by Lil Wayne, in November 2008.

Frank Ski, who had arguably been Baltimore club's biggest celebrity before K-Swift, flew up from Atlanta to DJ a fundraiser for K-Swift's family at the Iguana Cantina. One of K-Swift's closest friends and *Off the Hook* Radio co-host, Johnny "Porkchop" Doswell also spun at the Iguana, later remembering crying in the DJ booth as he played uptempo club tracks: "I'm standin' in the booth, everybody could see me, I cried all night long."

A month later, Porkchop and Supa DJ Big L paid tribute to K-Swift in a live broadcast from Club Choices, and emotions were still running high. "We ain't been down Choices together in a long time, L. We down here because our girl ain't here no more. Put a peace sign in the air for K-Swift!" Porkchop yelled on the mic during the broadcast. He led a call-and-response chant of her name before adding, "If I start crying, don't mind me, man. Just ventin'."

Less than two weeks after K-Swift's death, I sat down with eight past and present Club Queen Entertainment staffers.

Say Wut and his wife Crystal Tennessee hosted the gathering in their Sandtown home. I've never experienced the kind of outpouring of emotion I felt in their living room that day. The grief and lingering shock hung heavily over K-Swift's friends. Many of them had known her since her first club gigs at the Twilight Zone, and were with her the last weekend of her life, whether at Artscape or at the Friday night "My Crew Be Unruly" party at the Paradox. Some had been at her pool party on Sunday, leaving hours before her death.

"I haven't even mourned her yet, because I'm so pissed about how she died. It took me for her mother to call me the day after her funeral to tell me to stop blamin' myself," said Porkchop. "To this day, I think if I was at the house, that wouldn't have happened." Attendees of the party who witnessed her death had been eerily silent since that night, which fostered an atmosphere of suspicion and resentment. Some felt anger at the possibility that even if K-Swift's death was simply an accident with no foul play, more could've been done to administer possibly life-saving care in the minutes after she dove into the pool and sustained her fatal injuries. An autopsy found that K-Swift had died of a broken neck, with "a small amount of alcohol" and no drugs found in her bloodstream.

Jumpoff Vol. 14: The Queen Edition, released in March 2008, was the most recent K-Swift mix CD at the time of her death. Four months after the tragedy, Koch and Unruly announced that the first album under the labels' joint venture would be the posthumous release of the final mix that K-Swift had completed in her lifetime. K-Swift had planned *Jumpoff Greatest Hits, Vol. 1–5* as the first in a series of three CDs that would collect the best of her *Jumpoff* series, this one covering the 2004–2005 era.

"It was the last mix that she actually did. We were planning to release it right around when she passed. When she passed, we just pulled it back," Shawn Caesar told me at the time. "[Koch] never wavered, they never stopped, they were very respectful of the time that we needed to get through that, and never pushed anything. They were very very good about the whole situation, and we're very appreciative."

Since K-Swift had not recorded her usual spoken intros and outros for the disc before she died, an internationally famous artist who'd championed Baltimore club, M.I.A., was asked to host the album, which was released in early 2009. Rye Rye and one of K-Swift's frequent 92Q co-hosts, DJ Squirrel Wyde, also made appearances. Ultimately, *Greatest Hits* would be the only album to come out of Unruly's deal with Koch. "I think they wanted to see how it went, and then the timing was just so crazy and misfortunate, we just kept it there," Scottie B. says.

Unruly considered releasing a K-Swift DVD, but the project never came to fruition. "It's always hard to maneuver, because I'm always very very proud to present Swift to the world now, and I don't wanna overdo it," Shawn Caesar says.

Other DJs on the scene, particularly ones who specialized in making and selling mix CDs, had found K-Swift's success on the scene to be positive motivation. Chris Jones, better known as DJ Chris J., had been spinning club music since the early '90s. But he didn't get serious about producing his own tracks until Swift played his music on 92Q, where she popularized "Good Foot," better known as "The Aww Track" for its groaning wordless vocal loop.

"I didn't release anything to nobody. I kinda kept it to myself, because I wasn't sure. But then as I developed my sound and got more confident, I started leaking my tracks out, gave 'em to Swift, and she played 'em." Chris J., who'd worked at music stores like Dimensions In Music and Rod Lee's Club Kings outlet, released 22 volumes of his *Club Mix* series, and was at one point the only DJ besides K-Swift selling CDs on her website, ClubQueenKSwift.com. After her death, though, Chris J. stopped releasing mix CDs for several years. When he finally returned, 2015's *Club Going Up* was, naturally, dedicated to K-Swift. Sadly, DJ Chris J. also passed away in 2016. He was 35.

Similarly, DJ Frie was one of the scene's most prolific mix-CD creators until K-Swift's death, releasing 17 volumes of his *Da Club Tip* series. "Every month, like very first of the month, I'd have a new CD. Me and her was the only two that was doin' it. She'd do hers and I'd go, she'd have new stuff, I'd have new stuff. But when she passed away, I just, like, gave up," he said in November 2008. "Ain't nobody tryin' to take her spot."

In 2009, DJ Diamond K released *The K-Swift Story*, a 60-minute documentary featuring much of the available on-camera footage of K-Swift as well as interviews with her contemporaries. Sales of the DVD raised money for the DJ K-Swift Memorial Scholarship Fund. Two years after her death, 92Q held an event in Reedbird Park in Cherry Hill, declaring July 25th "K-Swift Day." Events that night at Skateworks and Bourbon Street donated admission charges to the scholarship fund.

The loss of K-Swift, as sudden and shocking as it was, left a mark on the scene, especially for those who knew her. "It's just too much, man," Porkchop said. "She gave everything to us." 92Q dubbed the booth she used to broadcast from "The K-Swift Memorial Mic Booth." Porkchop began spinning a nightly "Swift mix" on the station, always signing off his broadcasts with a passionate shout out: "K-Swift for-EVER!"

Porkchop released his own emotional tribute rap, "Never Be Another," selling physical copies of the song to give the proceeds to the Edgerton family. The best song posthumously inspired by K-Swift, however, would have to be K.W. Griff's "Pork and Swift," which features the familiar sound of Porkchop and K-Swift joking around and ad libbing on the radio, chopped up and set to a beat. In her absence, K-Swift's voice became another instrument in club tracks, her familiar laugh and "yeah yeah" ad libs skipping across breakbeats. In 2009, Griff made a sequel, "Swift's Revenge," which sampled one of the songs K-Swift played in her final Artscape set, M.I.A.'s "Boyz."

Not long ago, I turned on the radio and heard a Baltimore club set on a Washington, D.C., radio station, 95.5 WPGC, that included "Pork and Swift." Hearing those two voices bouncing back and forth at each other on that track always conjures up visceral memories of the years I spent listening to K-Swift and Porkchop laugh it up on the air, night after night. In that moment, I realized that WPGC was playing a song that featured three employees of a competing station, owned by a different company, in a different city. 15 years after her death, K-Swift's impact was still that strong.

Chapter 24

I'm the Ish

Three months after K-Swift's death, the co-founder of her label got an unexpected phone call that would help Unruly Records turn a corner after the tragedy. Shawn Caesar was in his office one day in early November 2008 when he heard from DJ Class, one of Unruly's first artists over a decade earlier. "DJ Class calls me like, 'Check your email, I sent you a song,'" Caesar says. "I open it up, and it's hot." Hot is an understatement. "I'm the Ish" was the one, the Baltimore club track that exploded upon impact like nothing since Rod Lee's "Dance My Pain Away."

Jay Claxton, who was working the afternoon shift at 92Q, doing the 5 o'clock mix in the station's peak rush-hour time slot, happened to be in Caesar's office at that moment, and wanted to put the song on the air ASAP. "So I hit Class back, and we get everything updated, took care of publishing and copyright, and the next day it's on," Caesar says.

Where most of Baltimore club's most enduring songs took months to build from clubs to nighttime radio spins, "I'm the Ish" jumped the line and went straight to daytime airplay. "I think one of the key components was the way that Jay went into it with the 5 o'clock mix, as opposed to necessarily playin' it late night," Class told me. Those circumstances certainly helped, but it was mostly that the track itself was irresistible. "I'm the shit up in this bitch" may have not been the most radio-friendly chorus, but a quick fix to "I'm this ish all up in here" got the point across and helped the song go further. "It's a whole different feel for Baltimore music, and anybody else can pop it in. The record's gonna cross over," Class accurately predicted weeks after the song was released.

Daniel "DJ Class" Woodis Jr., born in 1971, had been a pioneer of Baltimore club and active throughout the '90s. But he hadn't made any Baltimore club tracks since early 2000s hits like "Roc Da Bells" and "Next to You," and had spent a few years living in Atlanta and pivoting towards hip hop. He became the first and only Baltimore club artist to contribute music to a film by Baltimore icon John Waters, 2000's *Cecil B. Demented*. In 2006, he released a gospel rap album, *The Book of Daniel (The Hip Hop Testament)*, as D Class.

Class was missed in his time away. I first heard in 2006 that he'd moved to Atlanta from Dukeyman, who pointed to Class's absence as one reason that he was less excited about the scene than he used to be. "The stuff we had, like Class, he had one song that would play all year. And it hit, every time you play it, it would sound like it just came out," he said. "These songs now, they go in rotation for like a week." Further proving Dukeyman's point, "I'm the Ish" stayed in rotation for a long, long time.

Class had been part of the My Crew Be Unruly party at Paradox in July 2008, spinning with K-Swift two nights before her death. Perhaps that had provided some of the inspiration for Class to return to his hometown sound, but he came back with a few new tricks up his sleeve. He sampled the old "Think" break via a slightly different source: the 1988 Kid 'N Play single "Do This My Way," which didn't chart in America, but was the New York duo's biggest hit in the UK.

Then Class added some percussion accents that gave the track a new kind of shimmy, and sang through the pitch-correction software Auto-Tune on the maximum setting, which gave the human voice an eerie robotic sheen as it changed keys, a sound that Florida R&B star T-Pain had turned into a staple of American pop in the 2000s.

Of course, it mattered that it was a certified veteran of Baltimore club like DJ Class who helped give the genre a makeover for a new era. "I'm The Ish" could've been a hit coming from a younger producer, but it might not have had the same credibility to be embraced so widely by the city. "Now that club music's blowin' up, everybody's on the bandwagon that used to bash it," Jonny Blaze said. "Big ups to Class for that, Class did his thing, I gotta give him props, I'm glad it wasn't no new person."

By the end of November 2008, the song had spread to WPGC in Washington, D.C., WBLX in Mobile, Alabama, and KSMB in Lafayette, Louisiana. The first email blast that Unruly sent out to distribute "I'm The Ish" to DJs and the media boasted that the song was "from the forthcoming album *Alameda & Coldspring.*'" Plans were quickly made to release the album through Unruly's deal with Koch, which had recently rebranded as E1 Music. The song grew so quickly, though, that it felt like only a major label could handle it. So when Universal Republic came calling, Class signed a new deal with Unruly's full support.

"It started takin' on a life of its own, and we realized that we didn't have the resources to keep up with the record," Ceasar says. Part of the reason it felt like the right time for Baltimore club to finally storm the major-label world was that the genre had become more synth-heavy and less reliant on samples. "The music has kinda pushed itself forward a little bit. So we're cognizant of the samples, but there's nowhere near what it once was."

Universal signed Class just before the remixes started pouring in. That December, Caesar got a call from the manager of R&B star Trey Songz: Trey and rapper/producer Jermaine Dupri had just done a remix of "I'm The Ish" and were about to upload it to YouTube.

Lil Jon, the Atlanta producer whose sampled voice had been a constant presence on Baltimore club tracks for years, made his first official appearance on a Baltimore record in January 2009, when he went in the studio with DJ Class to make an official "I'm the Ish" remix. DJ Class was impressed to learn that Lil Jon was already familiar with his earlier music. "Come to find out he knows 'Next To You,' he knows 'NaNaNa.' He's a genius dude, he knows a lot about a lot of different areas of dance music, Baltimore club, Miami bass," DJ Class says. Still, Lil Jon didn't know just how much he had been sampled on Baltimore club songs until Class clued him in. "We talked about it, he thought it was one or two records, I was like, 'Oh, no, man.'"

Miami rap star Pitbull added a verse to the Lil Jon remix a few weeks after its initial release. Baltimore rappers Mullyman and PenDragon put together their own remixes as hometown excitement around the song reached a fever pitch. Local producers Da Yo Boyz released an "I'm the Ish" remix that mashed up Class's track with Atlanta rapper Gucci Mane's similarly themed 2008 song "I'm Da Shit."

In March 2009, the momentum went up another level yet again when rap superstar Kanye West remixed "I'm The Ish." West had recently become infatuated with Auto-Tune and released the album *808s & Heartbreak* in late 2008 to some of the most divided reviews of his career. The album absolutely dominated urban radio, though, overcoming skeptics to become a serious hit, not just the experimental detour it initially seemed to be.

By the time West jumped on "I'm the Ish," he was defiant and triumphant: "I dropped another album before we finished up the tour/ And it's still top 10 'bout 15 weeks later, so that's a middle finger for you *808* haters." The remix ended with Kanye West, perhaps the biggest star in music at that moment, singing a refrain of "crew be Unruly," repeating the name of Baltimore club's top label several times.

Although "I'm the Ish" did not break into *Billboard*'s main singles chart, the Hot 100, it appeared on the Bubbling Under chart, which features the next 20 songs just outside the top 100 singles in the country. It also did well on the Rap, Rhythmic, and Hot R&B/Hip-Hop Songs charts as the various remixes, particularly the Kanye West version, took the song national.

Pitbull was just beginning to become a mainstream star in 2009, and he returned to the studio with DJ Class several times after the "I'm The Ish" remix. Class produced "Juice Box," a full-scale Baltimore club track, on Pitbull's 2009 breakthrough album *Rebelution*. A year later, Class produced a single from Pitbull's first Spanish-language album, *Armando*, "Watagatapitusberry." And Pitbull's 2012 album *Global Warming* featured the DJ Class–produced Jennifer Lopez collaboration "Drinks For You (Ladies Anthem)," with J.Lo herself extensively quoting lyrics from "I'm The Ish" on the song's chorus.

In August 2024, Aaron LaCrate and All Surface Publishing filed a lawsuit against Pitbull over similarities between the "descending lines" of the synths on Debonair Samir's "Samir's Theme" and Pitbull's 2021 single "I Feel Good." LaCrate alleges that he sent the Samir track to Pitbull producer White Shadow and received positive feedback on it. The similarities are very slight, however, and given the fragile house of cards in which Baltimore club exists, with so many uncleared samples, it feels like bad artistic karma to file lawsuits like this.

Though Class's 2009 tracks "Dance Like A Freak" and "I Don't Give a Fuck" sounded like perfect follow-ups to "I'm the Ish" and kept his voice ubiquitous in Baltimore clubs, the momentum eventually dissipated, and Universal never released *Alameda & Coldspring*. Class had his foot in the door of the mainstream music industry, though, and has stayed there ever since in one way or another, including producing an official Baltimore club remix of Usher's chart-topping 2010 single "OMG."

One of DJ Class's old contemporaries from the '90s Unruly era, K.W. Griff, also came back big a year after "I'm The Ish" with a breakout hit.

The original concept for "Bring in the Katz" came from the song's vocalist, Johnny "Porkchop" Doswell. The track features Porkchop delivering a loose monologue that keeps building up to him barking the command, "Ay, Griff, bring in the katz!" followed by Griff cueing an uproarious stuttering sample that doesn't sound like cats, or like anything else you could guess. The song's inspired, infectious nonsense, difficult to decode even for the track's producer, was part of its appeal.

"Pork came to me with the idea of making a club track about 'Bring in the Katz.' I had no idea what he was talking about, but I wanted to hear him out," Griff told the dance magazine *XLR8R* for a feature about the best tracks of 2012, after a re-release of "Katz" by the British label Night Slugs helped the track find an international audience far outside Baltimore. "He went into the radio station and recorded all of his vocals in one take. He handed me the CD and said, 'Here are the vocals for the track. Work your magic!' We had no idea this track would spread across the coast the way it has."

Over a decade later, "Bring in the Katz" still goes off as probably the most popular Baltimore club track of the 2010s. "It's so powerful, to this day," Griff says.

Chapter 25
Shake It to the Ground

By the early 2010s, Blaqstarr had been on the cusp of the mainstream for quite a while. Tracks he'd produced for D.O.G., Young Leek, and M.I.A. were released on major labels. "Tote It," the song that kickstarted Blaqstarr's career when he sent it to K-Swift in 2003, was sampled by rap superstar Lil Wayne in 2009. Unfortunately, Lil Wayne's rise had been fueled by his ultra-prolific output, and dozens of songs leaked to the internet before they could be officially released, including the Blaqstarr-sampling "Told Y'all." The song appeared on unofficial mixtapes like *The Leak Reloaded*, but never got a retail release, and is only available on YouTube today.

As a solo artist, Blaqstarr evolved his sound quickly. His self-released 2006 mixtape *I'm Banging* was a highlight reel of his early Baltimore club hits. It also included lesser-known tracks like the brilliant "Check Me Out Like," featuring naggingly catchy synth riffs and a chop of the "Think" breakbeat that almost resembled the cadence of '90s drum'n'bass more than Baltimore club.

That song, as well as "Tote It" and other earlier tracks, reached a wider audience on Blaqstarr's first Mad Decent release, the *Supastarr* EP, gaining him much of his first significant press coverage outside Baltimore. An EPK (electronic press kit) was assembled by Mad Decent, a two-minute video biography of Blaqstarr to introduce him to media outlets and music retailers. The short film mostly showed footage of Blaqstarr performing in Baltimore, with occasional embarrassing touches like the words "HOOD BORN" flashing on the screen that seemed to exotify the producer's working-class Baltimore background.

Blaqstarr's teen rapper protégé Rye Rye made her debut on the Supastarr track "Shake It to the Ground." In fact, the EP featured two versions of the song: the main mix and an a cappella edit comprising only Rye Rye's vocals. A 12" single for "Shake It" boasted an instrumental mix, and remixes by a cross section of stars from the blog house and indie dance scenes: Switch & Santogold, Drop the Lime, Jokers of the Scene, and Claude VonStroke. But it was the wide availability of the a cappella version on the EP that really became the legacy of "Shake It."

Another track on the EP gave a hint of what was to come: "Rockstarrz" was a collaboration with James "Woody Rock" Green, a member of the Baltimore R&B group Dru Hill's original lineup. "Rockstarrz" was the first song that deployed the sound of Rye Rye saying the word "what" on "Shake It" as a disembodied loop. It functioned more like a percussion instrument than a human voice, which became the model for how countless other producers would integrate the Rye Rye "what" into tracks in the future.

M.I.A. took particular interest in Rye Rye, bringing her on tour as an opening act in the UK and the United States. The Baltimore teenager made a cameo in the video for the *Kala* single "Paper Planes," and appeared on a remix of the track alongside Nigerian rapper Afrikan Boy. The *Paper Planes – Homeland Security Remixes* EP, which included a full-on Baltimore club remix by Scottie B., was released in February 2008, a few months before prominent placement in the film

Pineapple Express helped "Paper Planes" become a surprise mainstream hit, going all the way to #4 on the Hot 100.

Rye Rye soon became the first artist that M.I.A. signed to her Interscope imprint N.E.E.T. Recordings, and the two collaborated on the thunderous Blaqstarr-produced single "Bang," which appeared on the soundtrack album for 2009 action film *Fast & Furious* and was remixed by DJ Booman. Rye Rye's 2009 mixtape *Blaqout* was entirely produced by Blaqstarr, a 33-minute montage of rhymes and hooks over club beats, heavily featuring his own tracks alongside promising previews of Rye Rye's N.E.E.T. album like the frantic "I Run This."

Rye Rye was on a rapid rise, but that trajectory was soon complicated by the 18-year-old rapper becoming a mother. Female rappers have often had to deal with biological realities that can impact their careers in ways that their male counterparts seldom experience, particularly pregnancy and motherhood. Superstars like Lauryn Hill and Cardi B became pregnant while working on their debut albums, and M.I.A. herself famously performed while nine months pregnant at the 2009 Grammys alongside Jay-Z, Kanye West, Lil Wayne, and T.I.

The Blaqstarr-produced 2009 version of Rye Rye's debut album was an unfortunate casualty of N.E.E.T.'s plans changing after the rapper's pregnancy. She eventually recorded a very different set of songs that would see release three years later.

Rye Rye finally had her grand coming-out party on a national stage in 2012 with not just an album release but also her feature film debut. In March of that year, Rye Rye played a supporting role in the box office hit *21 Jump Street*, recording the film's theme song with Esthero. Two months later, she released *Go! Pop! Bang!*, the first major-label album by a Baltimore rapper since B. Rich's Atlantic album *80 Dimes,* almost a decade earlier.

"I always had, like, halfway support within the city," Rye Rye told me shortly after performing at an album release event at the Fells Point record store Sound Garden. "I'm not worrying about that stuff, or whether the whole city supporting me, because I had buzz outside of the city. I still put on for Baltimore, but I'm moving forward."

Go! Pop! Bang! had a serious pop pedigree, with guest appearances by big names like Akon and Robyn, and production from RedOne (Lady Gaga, Nicki Minaj) and the Neptunes. For better or worse, the Neptunes' "Shake Twist Drop" beat did not continue the Baltimore club homage phase that Pharrell Williams had begun on Twista's "Give It Up."

The only beats on the album by Blaqstarr, or anyone from Baltimore, were the years-old songs "Shake It to the Ground" and "Bang," which appeared as bonus tracks on a deluxe edition. Blaqstarr was still proud to see Rye Rye get her moment in the spotlight, telling me, "It's actually a beautiful thing, [like seeing] a family member graduate." *Go! Pop! Bang!* was warmly reviewed by *Rolling Stone* and *Pitchfork* but sold modestly, missing the *Billboard* 200 and peaking at #23 on the Rap Albums chart and #12 on the Dance/Electronic Albums chart.

In 2024, some hard feelings about Rye Rye's N.E.E.T. tenure bubbled to the surface when M.I.A. vented on X (the social network formerly known as Twitter) about a custody battle over her daughter, posting, "I sacrificed my career for my child." In response, Rye Rye posted, "But you wanted me to sacrifice my kid for my career. You was calling me while I'm dealing with my child father shot up in a bed trying [to] get me to get an abortion at 6 months."

In the years after K-Swift's death, Blaqstarr had drifted away from Baltimore club both musically and personally, moving to Los Angeles and shifting towards less-danceable downtempo music. The 2010 *Divine* EP featured acoustic songs like "Wonder Woman" and a remix of "Ryda Gyrl" (as "Rider Girl") with completely different drums that just about removed any trace of Baltimore club from the song.

"She Is Love" – a guitar-driven pop song that *Spin*'s Marc Hogan compared to Outkast's Andre 3000 circa "Hey Ya!" – was released in summer 2012 as the lead single from a Blaqstarr album titled *Here We Are*, which was to be released by N.E.E.T./ Interscope. The next time I saw Blaqstarr, in late 2013, he'd come back home after marrying a Baltimore girl he'd met in L.A. They were expecting their first child, he was releasing more music with Mad Decent, working on a myriad of other independent projects, and the once-announced Interscope album didn't come up in our conversation. I'd forgotten about it, and maybe he had, too. N.E.E.T. folded in 2018 without having released the Blaqstarr album, or a follow up to Rye Rye's album.

Upon returning to Baltimore, Blaqstarr worked with a younger club producer, the ascendant Mighty Mark, then known as Murder Mark, on the track "Turn Down for What." But much of his work continued to be unpredictable and exploratory, including live performances with an acoustic guitar under the name Jamal Loving (a combination of his middle name and his mother's maiden name). He was still interested in at least preserving his piece of Baltimore club history, though, remastering his early work for *The Blaq-Files (2002–06)* EP, released on Mad Decent in 2014.

Over the last decade, Rye Rye's ad libs from "Shake It to

the Ground," particularly the loop of her saying "what," have become a part of the standard kit of sounds employed by producers in both the Baltimore club scene and the heavily Baltimore-influenced Jersey club scene. Rye Rye continued releasing independent singles, often collaborating with newer producers who were fans of her early work. DJ Dizzy, from the Baltimore suburb Edgewood, sampled the Rye Rye "what" alongside Rye Rye's newly recorded verses on "Hips For Me," as did New Jersey's DJ Joker 106 on "Move 2 Da Beat," both tracks released in 2023.

In 2022, the Toronto rapper Drake, a Lil Wayne protégé who'd subsequently become a massive superstar in his own right, followed his mentor in sampling Baltimore club on his house music–influenced album *Honestly, Nevermind*. Diamante Anthony Blackmon, a dance DJ/producer known as Gordo, co-produced four tracks on the album that frequently featured Baltimore kick-drum patterns, including "Currents," which sampled Rye Rye's "what."

Gordo, who grew up an hour outside Baltimore in Frederick, Maryland, posted to X about his club music homage the day that *Honestly, Nevermind* was released to an unsuspecting public who'd never heard Drake rap on fast-paced house beats before: "Baltimore club music was always being played in the car by my mother and the family… felt good to bring it to the masses on this album." Rye Rye, for her part, seemed flattered but also disappointed that she wasn't credited or compensated for the sample. Blaqstarr, perhaps sensing an opportunity, released another collection of remixed early work called *Blaq to the Basics* just four days after *Honestly, Nevermind*.

A year later, Drake released a new album, *For All the Dogs*. The track "Calling for You," featuring 21 Savage, once again contained the Rye Rye "what" sample without attribution, though it was not produced by Gordo or anyone else with known Maryland roots.

On Instagram, a member of Drake's OVO label team, Mr. Morgan, celebrated the release of *For All the Dogs* in a post that contained text messages from the making of the album in which he was asked, "Did you clear the sample?" and replied with a whimsical meme that implied he had not (Rye Rye was not the only artist who said they were sampled or interpolated on the album without credit or permission). This time, Rye Rye seemed more actively irritated. "MY VOCALS AGAIN? & NO CREDIT?," she posted on X. "But thank you for reminding me that my 15-year-old vocals are still legendary. This is not funny, this sent me into a deep depression and made me angry inside the first time. Now I gotta relive this again."

In 2024, Kid Cudi followed in Drake's footsteps with "Babe And I," a Baltimore club–influenced track that featured Rye Rye's uncredited vocal sample. That same year, London singer Jordan Adetunji released "Kehlani," a hit single named after California R&B star Kehlani, and the song featured a loop of Rye Rye's "what." "Kehlani" peaked at No. 24 on the Hot 100, making it the third year in a row that Rye Rye's voice appeared on a top-40 hit following "Currents" (No. 23) and "Calling for You" (No. 5).

Another example of the erasure of Baltimore's influence on contemporary club music is Florida beatmaker Jarvis "JRitt" Rittman's hit "Benjamins Deli," which racked up over seven million plays on TikTok, with celebrities like Jimmy Fallon participating in the viral dance challenge. JRitt's track was named after its two most recognizable mainstream samples of songs by New York rappers: Puff Daddy's 1997 smash "It's All About the Benjamins," and rising star Ice Spice's recent hit "Deli." But the track features a third sample that might not be so familiar to many: Blaqstarr's voice from "Get My Gun." Even JRitt himself seemed ignorant of the Baltimore origins of the sample, tagging his track as "#jerseyclub" when he first posted it. On almost every occasion that Baltimore club has touched the mainstream in recent years, Jersey club has gotten most of the credit.

Baltimore rapper Tate Kobang, whose given name is Joshua Goods, was born in the early '90s and grew up steeped in Baltimore club music. A younger cousin to club music legend Dukeyman, Tate Kobang's profile rose in 2015 when he decided to look back to one of the hometown anthems of his youth, the Tim Trees classic "Bank Roll," sampling one of Rod Lee's first hip hop productions. Tate Kobang liked to release music on April 19th to commemorate his late mother's birthday, putting his version of "Bank Roll" on YouTube that day as a freebie to promote his album *Live Hazey*.

April 19th, 2015, was a significant day in Baltimore for other reasons. A 25-year-old man named Freddie Gray died of injuries sustained a week earlier in custody of Baltimore city police. His death was ruled a homicide by medical examiners, and prosecutors filed criminal charges against six police officers. Baltimoreans took to the streets in massive Black Lives Matter protests against police brutality, and Maryland's Republican governor, Larry Hogan, deployed the National Guard in Baltimore.

The original Tim Trees track had come out when Tate Kobang was only eight years old, and it symbolized a happy, nostalgic memory for him and other Baltimoreans of his generation. "If 'Bank Roll' come on, it makes you feel good," Kobang told me that year. "And that's what we're tryin' to do, put some fun back into the city, because Baltimore is depressing right now."

"I've been a G since kiddie discos at the Hammerjacks," Kobang rapped on "Bank Rolls (Remix)," reminiscing about the Easter all-ages club music parties at the storied downtown venue. The song racked up a buzz so big that Kobang was signed to 300 Entertainment by Kevin Liles, the veteran label executive whose music industry career began in Baltimore with Numarx. "'We finally got someone from Baltimore that we can put chips into,'" Kobang remembers Liles telling him.

Kobang expanded "Bank Rolls (Remix)" into a full-length song with the help of the track's original producer, Rod Lee. "I said, 'We gotta make a song, it's just a verse,'" Rod Lee says. "He came over to the crib, we recorded it."

Tate Kobang worked on a debut album for 300 Entertainment with mainstream hip hop hitmakers like Honorable C.N.O.T.E., but also kept the influence of Baltimore club in the mix to rep his hometown. Dukeyman engineered the sessions, and Blaqstarr produced multiple tracks. "Me and Blaqstarr got some shit," Kobang told me. "But the thing is, the world's not ready for Blaqstarr, so you can't give them too much." Ultimately, the world wasn't ready for Kobang either, and the album was shelved as he eventually parted ways with 300.

Within a few years, however, Kobang worked his way further up the music industry ladder, working with major stars as a producer and songwriter. In 2020, he co-wrote the top-10 hit "Mr. Right Now" by 21 Savage and Metro Boomin featuring Drake. In 2022, he had a hand in creating the song that eventually became Beyonce's "Virgo's Groove." In 2023, Tate Kobang signed with Nicki Minaj's Heavy On It label, working on six tracks on Minaj's chart-topping album *Pink Friday 2*. Minaj's Lil Uzi Vert collaboration "Everybody" was co-produced by Kobang and New Jersey's DJ Smallz 732.

"Catching records that's in the vein of what you came up on, that shit make you proud of your upbringing," Kobang told the *Baltimore Banner* in 2023. "I grew up on club." Kobang also produced Baltimore rap star YG Teck's 2024 single "Bomb," which put a Baltimore club spin on one of the biggest songs ever to come out of the city: Sisqo's 2000 smash "Thong Song."

Aside from the DJ Class–produced 2000 remix of "Got to Get It," Sisqo had never made a Baltimore club song until 2022, when he appeared on the NBC reality show "American Song Contest." The series, inspired by the Eurovision Song Contest, featured an artist from each of the 50 states, with mostly unknown musicians going up against a few home-state heroes like Jewel, representing Alaska, and Sisqo, representing Maryland.

"I'm showcasing Baltimore club music with my song on this show," Sisqo proudly announced before performing his contest entry "It's Up." Unfortunately, the track wasn't produced by any established local beatmaker from the club scene, and was neither a credible attempt at the Baltimore club sound nor a hit with the national viewing audience. Sisqo was quickly eliminated from "American Song Contest," and "It's Up" never made it into his top 10 songs on Spotify.

"Whores in This House," the profane classic Frank Ski released in 1992, wound up infiltrating pop culture more than just about any Baltimore club track over the next three decades. OutKast's Big Boi quoted it on the group's 1996 song "Ova Da Wudz." Rappers Joe Budden and Busta Rhymes and producer Just Blaze, all from New Jersey, interpolated "Whores" on the 2003 single "Fire (Yes, Yes Y'all)." The Budden song wasn't a significant hit, but it appeared in the 2004 movie *Mean Girls*, which represented the first time that the vocalist and co-producer of "Whores," Al "T" McLaran, received credit and publishing for his work on the song. Lil Wayne's "Whores" homage, "In This House" with Gucci Mane, appeared as a bonus track on 2018's *Tha Carter V.*

In August 2020, two of the most famous rappers in the country, New York's Cardi B and Houston's Megan Thee Stallion, released "WAP," a collaboration that debuted at #1 on the Hot 100. The sound of McLaran's voice saying, "There's some whores in this house" is looped 79 times on "WAP," a song that sent shockwaves through American news media with its unapologetic celebration of "wet-ass pussy."

Frank Ski was listed as one of the six co-writers of "WAP," but McLaran was not. I called him in Florida the day after the Cardi B track was released, and McLaran was diplomatic about the situation. "I spoke to [Frank], we're cool. We were all young then and things just weren't handled the way they should have been handled," McLaran said. Today, "WAP" has well over one billion streams on Spotify, but McLaran is still not credited as a writer on it. The original "Whores in This House" is not available on Spotify at all, perhaps the ultimate example of how Baltimore club's history is remembered, but not preserved.

Antonio "DJ Turito" Lord comes from a family full of DJs – "There are, like, seven of us" – and is a seasoned musician and multi-instrumentalist who just started DJing a few years ago. "I'm from New York originally, so I've always been big on house music," says DJ Turito.

DJ Turito, who was born in 1980, loves Baltimore club music. He plays it in his sets whenever he gets the chance, but he tends to book gigs where he plays Caribbean and African genres, not Baltimore club.

"That's been one of the hardest scenes to actually get into, because I've spoken to a couple of club or house DJs that I know, and they've all said the same thing: it's a very tight knit group. Once you get the nod of approval, then they'll start letting you in. But to find some of these events hasbeen very difficult, to be honest with you."

Once upon a time, DJs and producers could only mix or sample sections of a track with all the instruments present at once – if a 12" single featured instrumental and a cappella versions, then you could mix the beat and vocal separately, but that was often as much one could do to select individual elements of a song. Recent advancements in technology, however, allow a DJ to separate a song into "stems." You can isolate just the drums, or the just the bassline, or just the vocal, as if you had the song's original studio files. "Now that we can mess with the stems on Serato and VirtualDJ, I find myself mixing the old rhythms with new ones," says Turito.

Turito's experiments with stems have led him to mix and match elements of '90s Baltimore club with radically different styles. "I'll use Miss Tony, Dukeyman, 'Pick 'Em Up,' I'll take some of those, and then I'll probably take the vocals off and sometimes I'll blend Afro house rhythms, so I might take one of the old songs and put 'em over a Black Coffee rhythm." Baltimore club emerged out of fusing different genres together, but now it has its own distinct identity that can be fused with wholly different sounds from other continents.

American racial inequality has always been even more deeply felt in Baltimore than in other parts of the country, including disparities in healthcare. The life expectancy for Black Americans is over three years shorter than for White Americans, and the gap between Black Marylanders and White Marylanders widens to nearly five years.

Sadly, that means that many Baltimore club music legends have passed away far too young from health issues in the decades since Miss Tony's death from kidney failure at 36. Reggie Reg died of congestive heart failure in 2016 at the age of 50. Baltimore's then-mayor, Stephanie Rawlings-Blake, called him "one of the best DJs of my generation, with a personality bigger than life."

Jimmy Jones was also 50 when he died of kidney failure at Baltimore Good Samaritan Hospital on February 16, 2021. Jones was mourned by a wife and four kids, as well as a generation of local clubgoers. "Everybody in the clubs loved him," Booman told the *Baltimore Sun* for an obituary piece. "There were only a handful of people who did what he did so effectively. He had a good, strong voice and he connected with people."

Ron "Dukeyman" Hall Jr. suffered a stroke and passed away at 50 years old on February 16, 2024 – three years to the day after Jimmy Jones's death. Dukeyman may have lost his passion for making Baltimore club tracks in the early 2000s, but he remained a vital and beloved part of the club music community in the last two decades of his life. He ran a label, Music Madness Records, and a record pool, MMRP. He took up graphic design and started designing party flyers and mix CD covers for friends like DJ Kenny K. And he was a gifted gear head who wouldn't hesitate to help other DJs and producers out. "I called him all the time, any software, any piece of gear, 'Oh yeah, I got it, come get it, take it to y'all house, see how you like it.' He was that type of guy, all the time," says DJ Booman.

At the time of Jimmy Jones's death, the Minneapolis-based platinum rapper/singer Lizzo had already begun incorporating his biggest song, "Watch Out for the Big

Girl," into her choreography routine on tour. About a year after Jones's death, Amazon Prime debuted the reality show "Lizzo's Watch Out for the Big Grrrls," in which 13 women competed to become a backup dancer for Lizzo. Jones's signature song was right out front, not just as the title, but also as the theme song of the series, which won three Emmy awards in September 2022. Booman re-released the track, proudly carrying on his fallen friend's legacy and shouting him out in frequent Facebook posts: "Rest in power, Jimmy Jones, we making it a movie down here for you!"

Five months after Jones's death in July 2021, the street where he grew up, on the corner of Harford and Fenwick Avenue, was renamed Jimmy Jones Way. "He will be with us forever," his sister Shontelle Jones told WJZ reporters.

In September 2024, a similar ceremony was held for one of the other Doo Dew Kidz. But this time, DJ Booman was alive to see a stretch of the Alameda at the intersection with Ednor Road renamed DJ Booman Way. It was a cool, windy day, but the rain let up that afternoon as dozens of friends and admirers and peers gathered to celebrate the occasion with Booman and his family, blocks away from where Booman and Griff grew up and made many of their early classics. K.W. Griff, Scottie B., DJ Kool Breez, Diamond K, and other club vets showed up for the ceremony.

In 2016, the block of North Avenue where Odell's stood was renamed Wayne Davis Way. In 2023, a block of Wadsworth Way was renamed Bossman Way in honor of the Baltimore rapper whose biggest hit was a Rod Lee–produced track with a "Think" breakbeat. Little by little, the map of Baltimore is changing to reflect club music's impact on the city.

Chapter 26
Reunions

"Hold the fuck up, Scottie, hold the fuck up!"

Emmanuel "DDm" Moss was standing onstage, performing Miss Tony's "Pull Ya Gunz Out" in front of two icons of Baltimore club music: Scottie B. working the turntables, and the Paradox sign bearing the club's logo on the wall behind the stage. DDm was asking Scottie to cut the beat for dramatic effect so he could admonish the audience that they need to go harder. "Bitches is keepin' it cute, but we in the motherfuckin' Dox, bitch!"

We weren't really in the Paradox. It was a May 2024 event called One Night at the Dox, and the real Paradox, located three miles away, had been closed for eight years. Of course, if it both is and isn't the Paradox, that's a nice paradox in and of itself, a fitting tribute to Wayne Davis's original inspiration for naming his club. And for one night, we all danced and celebrated like the Dox was back. Davis was in the house at the Lafayette Avenue venue known as the Garage, giving Larry "Whaddup" Caudle's event the official co-sign. Earlier in the week, Caudle posted a promotional video on social media holding the Paradox sign after borrowing it. "Had to go pick up the infamous sign. Wayne Davis, thank you big homie!"

"Reunion" events like this have become common in Baltimore – club nights billed as an "Odell's reunion" or

"Choices reunion," held in completely different contemporary venues, where the DJs and dancers of a bygone era can get together and turn back the clock, dancing all night to their favorite club music and house tracks.

One Night at the Dox also featured the original Paradox's legendary sound system, with throbbing bass that felt like it could punch a hole through your chest. Davis hasn't run a club since the Paradox closed in 2015, though not for lack of trying. "After Paradox closed, Ultra Nate and I were gonna partner and find a smaller venue to do something, like maybe a 300-person scale. But we ran into so many obstacles trying to find a space, it just kinda fell to the side," he says. The system is still available if somebody wanted it, but it's bulkier than modern club speakers, making it a tough sell. "I have all that stuff stored in a container, that sound system. The challenge now is getting rid of it, because it's so large, and everybody has gone to much smaller-scaled stuff."

DDm (short for Dappa Dan Midas) has emerged as something of a de facto caretaker of Miss Tony's legacy. A seasoned battle rapper, DDm came out of the closet in 2011 and became Baltimore's first openly gay rapper of note, opening some new doors for LGBTQ+ acceptance in Baltimore while also walking through some doors that Miss Tony had opened in the '90s. "I went through this period where everything I did, no matter how good it was, it was always 'gay rapper yada yada,'" DDm told me after he began to embrace his identity and appear at Baltimore Pride parades. "I think that now, especially the way the whole gay rights movement is going, I'd rather be an advocate through just living." DDm performed his first Miss Tony tribute set at Baltimore Pride in 2012, and it remains a tradition he's continued now and again for special occasions.

DDm has his own career and usually performs original material, but when he's drafted to carry it for Miss Tony and perform "How U Wanna Carry It," he gives it his all. For One Night at the Dox, DDm performed Tony's autobiographical tale of homelessness, "Living in the Alley," with an emotional intro noting his gratitude that he's now older than Miss Tony was when he died.

Say Wut, Rod Lee, and others took shifts behind the decks, while Buck Jones was the consummate club MC, even doing his uncanny impression of K-Swfit's trademark "Yeah yeah." As a furious dance circle emerged in the middle of the crowd during Say Wut's run of mid-2000s anthems, Jones free-associated on the mic: "Get in the circle, get in the oval… If you can't get in the O, you gotta go."

Caudle organized One Night at the Dox to follow the nearby Maryland Film Festival screening of *More Than Hype*, a documentary he directed about Baltimore club music. It's the third Baltimore club documentary, following Diamond K's 2009 DVD release, *The K-Swift Story*, and rapper TT The Artist's streaming release, *Dark City Beneath the Beat*. TT's film combined interviews with dazzling music video–style performance sequences. It was released on Netflix and executive produced by film and television star Issa Rae. As I was finishing this book, Chris Burley, younger brother of DJ Booman, was beginning work on another documentary project about Baltimore club music.

Caudle played host for much of One Night at the Dox, but he also spent more time dancing than almost anybody else in the building, shaking his legs with impressively precise chaos, even after the bar stopped serving drinks at 2am. Caudle attempted to pass the microphone to Wayne Davis and Shawn Caesar to give two legends of the Paradox era a moment in the spotlight, but neither seemed eager to give a speech and both quickly handed the mic back.

One of the most enjoyable aspects of the night was seeing the young stars of previous eras all grown up. Big Ria, now in her forties, performed her timeless roll call of neighborhood shoutouts from Diamond K's "Hey U Knuckleheads." A 34-year-old Hollywood Leek flew out from the West Coast to relive his days as the 15-year-old Young Leek who set Baltimore on fire with "Jiggle It" one summer. Deuce Tre Deuce, another group of teen K-Swift protégés, made an onstage cameo, but didn't perform their hit "Hands Up, Thumbs Down."

Baltimore City councilman Nick Mosby took a night off from his endless procession of corruption and financial scandals to put in an enthusiastic appearance at One Night at the Dox to try to appear relatable, remembering his younger days at the Paradox. Later that year, his bid for a second term as the city council president failed.

Mosby was born in 1978, and the 53rd Mayor of Baltimore, Brandon Scott, was born in 1984. They represent the first generation of city leadership that actually grew up with Baltimore club music, and the genre finally started to receive some overdue institutional acknowledgement under Scott's first term.

June 17, 2023, marked the first ever Baltimore Club Music Day, coinciding with Baltimore's annual African-American Festival (AFRAM). Shawn Caesar, Scottie B., DJ Class, DJ Technics, Frank Ski, DJ Patrick, K.W. Griff, Diamond K, Wayne Davis, DJ Booman, DJ Equalizer, and Karizma were officially designated as "the pioneers" of Baltimore club for the event, and several other producers and DJs received awards of recognition.

Meagan "Ducky Dynamo" Buster, a millennial DJ,

had become something of a Baltimore club historian and preservationist over the past decade, and thought the Baltimore city government could and should honor Baltimore club's cultural legacy in the same ways Washington, D.C,. had long done for go-go music.

"I carried on and was an advocate for what I see as the future of our city government's involvement in cultural stuff in general," Ducky Dynamo says.

> "I started essentially just messaging the mayor and trying to get an official sitdown with him on the city council calendar about starting an office of nightlife entertainment. At the same time that this was happening, DJ Class and Shawn Caesar had a similar idea, and they had the idea of a club music day."

Eventually they pooled their efforts together, and Baltimore Club Music Day came to fruition.

"It was cool, it was real cool," says Scottie B., who helped coordinate with the mayor's office to make sure club's legends were properly recognized. "I wanted to make sure everybody got their credit, because there was already a whole bunch of, 'Well I better get something something.' I was like, "If they had a song out on anything, or they were a DJ, they get an award, and we can just work from there.""

For many of the club vets who hadn't seen each other in years, Club Music Day was a joyful reunion. "I ran into Equalizer, I hadn't seen Equalizer in I don't know how long, a long time," Booman says.

It was also an opportunity for onetime competitors to set aside old grudges and bask in their collective accomplishments. "I kept pushing to make sure to include [DJ] Patrick, even though me and Patrick have had our issues, issues that we never should have had," Scottie B. says, showing a little emotion beneath his usually stoic exterior. "He come up here and he got a son. I don't even know that, you know what I mean? I'm supposed to know that. But we've just been lost in the sauce for so long. So I was happy to see him, glad to meet his son."

Ducky Dynamo hoped that the second Baltimore Club Music Day would be just as momentous as the first, but the mayor's office had other plans. 2024's AFRAM featured a celebration of Baltimore's house music legacy, honoring the Basement Boys. With no official Baltimore Club Music Day events put on by the city, Ducky Dynamo threw a cookout party and invited everyone she knew in the scene, hatching the idea to carry the torch herself, even if City Hall wouldn't. A few months later, Mayor Scott announced that the next Baltimore Club Day had been scheduled for April 8, 2025, the mayor's own birthday.

These days, a lot of '90s Baltimore club producers are still producing tracks, but many of them, like DJ Booman and Rod Lee, have been embracing their house music roots more and more. "It's more subtle, because look at it, we're getting' old. Can't jump around to this shit no more," Lee says. "You get tired, so y'know, slow the pace down a little bit so they can still reminisce and groove to it." Baltimore club still gets airtime on 92Q, particularly on the morning show hosted by two club music veterans, DJ Quicksilva and Porkchop, even if the classics get more spins than new tracks.

There are, however, younger producers still hitting their stride. Marquis "Mighty Mark" Gasque, born in 1989, started to impact the scene in 2007, and his breakthrough "Pump This Party" was one of the last new records that DJ K-Swift broke. "I was producing first and then moved into DJing just because the demand out-of-state called for it, people started saying, 'Hey, we wanna book you in New York to play your music,'" he says.

When he first made his name, Gasque was known as Murder Mark. "I was called Murder Mark from battle rapping, I used to battle rap in high school," he says. In 2014, he made the name-change to the superhero-inspired Mighty Mark, casting off the unintentional association with Baltimore's once famous murder rate, which has seen a notable decline under Mayor Scott's administration. "The connotation of Murder Mark can kind of put you in a box, it is a kind of negative thing." He's remained one of the scene's younger leading lights, and in 2024, he got the opportunity to start DJing at Camden Yards, playing Baltimore club music during Orioles games.

In May 2024, Ducky Dynamo posted a fundraising page on the website GoFundMe, "Join Ducky in Preserving Baltimore Club & Culture." The top priority of the project was to attempt to buy the building on the 1800 block of North Charles street that had held a historic place in Baltimore nightlife for half a century. In 1972, it had been Carousel, the first club owned by Odell Brock that Wayne Davis DJed at, and after that it became Gatsby's, and later Club Choices. If things go right, it may have an active dancefloor again, and could become a space where club music's history has a permanent home.

The genre's legends have also started to receive some prestigious invitations. DJ Booman has done speaking engagements at the Baltimore Museum of Art, the Eubie Blake National Jazz and Cultural Center, and the Reginald F. Lewis Museum. "I did a 30-minute presentation and broke down some of the records and the samples," Booman says. "They were talking about planning something at the Smithsonian too, it's pretty cool." After decades as one city's dirty little secret, Baltimore club music is recognized as high art in some of America's highest cultural institutions.

Bibliography

P. 10

"Odell Brock, Jr., 39, dies of cancer; was former owner of Odell's disco." The Baltimore Sun, December 16, 1984.
https://www.newspapers.com/article/the-baltimore-sun-odell-brock-dies/29412689/?locale=en-US

P. 15

Gunts, Ed. "Odell Brock's family holds a reunion to celebrate restoration of the historic Odell's building on North Avenue." Baltimore Fishbowl, November 24, 2021.
https://baltimorefishbowl.com/stories/odell-brocks-family-holds-a-reunion-to-celebrate-restoration-of-the-historic-odells-building-on-north-avenue/

Shipley, Al. "Teddy Douglas and DJ Exclaime talk this weekend's Respekt party at Paradox." Baltimore City Paper, October 26, 2012.
https://web.archive.org/web/20121031054806/http://blogs.citypaper.com/noise/index.php/2012/10/teddy-douglas-and-dj-exclaime-talk-this-weekends-respekt-party-at-paradox/

P. 16

Shipley, Al. "The Club Beat with DJ Kenny K and DJ Mike Crosby." Baltimore City Paper, February 17, 2011.
https://web.archive.org/web/20110223003333/http://blogs.citypaper.com/noise/index.php/2011/02/the-club-beat-with-dj-kenny-k-and-dj-mike-crosby/

Kladko, Brian and David Simon. "Narcotics suspect's disco seized by federal agents." The Baltimore Sun, December 4, 1987.
https://www.newspapers.com/article/the-baltimore-sun-odells-new-owner-is-a/29412916/

P. 17

"The trouble with Odell's." The Baltimore Sun, July 15, 1992.
https://www.baltimoresun.com/1992/07/15/the-trouble-with-odells/

"FBI raids Odell's, seizes documents." The Baltimore Sun, September 2, 1992.
https://www.baltimoresun.com/1992/09/02/fbi-raids-odells-seizes-documents-2/

"FBI raid at Odell's said to be part of corruption probe, club figure's dealings with officials questioned." The Baltimore Sun, September 6, 1992.
https://www.baltimoresun.com/1992/09/06/fbi-raid-at-odells-said-to-be-part-of-corruption-probe-club-figures-dealings-with-officials-questioned-2/

P. 19

"BV1103FILMS Presents: An Interview with DJ Technics."
YouTube video, October 19, 2023.
https://www.youtube.com/watch?v=VbppAd7w_VQ

P. 24

Shipley, Al. "The Club Beat with DJ Equalizer." Baltimore City
Paper, June 12, 2007.
http://www.citypaper.com/digest.asp?id=13726

Burney, Lawrence. "Scottie B: Baltimore Club 101." True
Laurels, June 30, 2014.
https://www.truelaurels.com/blog/2014/6/30/baltimore-
club-101-with-scottie-b

P. 35

Limbong, Andrew. "The Voice Behind One of Hip-Hop's Most
Famous Hooks." NPR Morning Edition, September 18, 2018.
https://www.npr.org/2018/09/18/648850102/the-voice-
behind-one-of-hip-hops-most-famous-hooks

Pappas, Breck. "The Amazing Life of Jabo Starks." Mobile
Bay Magazine, September 9, 2015.
https://mobilebaymag.com/the-amazing-life-of-jabo-starks/

P. 38

Host, Vivian. "Sing Sing: A Loop History." Red Bull Music
Academy, July 9, 2014.

https://daily.redbullmusicacademy.com/2014/07/sing-sing-a-loop-history

P. 40
Shipley, Al. "25 Years of Baltimore Club." Boiler Room, September 12, 2014.
https://legacy.boilerroom.tv/25-years-of-baltimore-club/

P. 44
Embert, Casey. "We Made All This Shit! The History of Unruly Records." The Baltimore Sun, June 21, 2016.
https://www.baltimoresun.com/2016/06/21/we-made-all-this-shit-the-history-of-unruly-records-which-just-celebrated-20-years-tells-the-history-of-baltimore-club-music/

P 59
McCabe, Bret. "Man of the House: For four decades Wayne Davis has shown that to build a club you start with the music." The Baltimore Sun, June 21, 2016.
https://www.baltimoresun.com/2016/06/21/man-of-the-house-for-four-decades-wayne-davis-has-shown-that-to-build-a-club-you-start-with-the-music/

P. 67
Shipley, Al. "The Story Behind 'WAP''s 'Whores in This House' Sample." Vulture, August 10, 2020.
https://www.vulture.com/2020/08/wap-whores-in-this-house-sample-explained.html

P 73

Shipley, Al. "The Club Beat with Jimmy Jones." Baltimore City Paper, September 26, 2008.
https://web.archive.org/web/20081004184356/http://www.citypaper.com/digest.asp?id=16763

Kelly, Jacques. "Jimmy Jones, Baltimore club musician known for 'Watch Out for the Big Girl,' dies." The Baltimore Sun, February 19, 2021.
https://www.baltimoresun.com/2021/02/19/jimmy-jones-baltimore-club-musician-known-for-watch-out-for-the-big-girl-dies/

P. 81

Murray, Shanon. "Running a new route: Records. Ravens wide receiver Michael Jackson is opening a record production company as a way of giving back to the Baltimore community." The Baltimore Sun, August 27, 1997.
https://www.baltimoresun.com/1997/08/27/running-a-new-route-records-ravens-wide-receiver-michael-jackson-is-opening-a-record-production-company-as-a-way-of-giving-back-to-the-baltimore-community-music-industry/

P. 83

Shipley, Al. "The Club Beat with DJ Manny." Baltimore City Paper, June 27, 2009.
http://www.citypaper.com/digest.asp?id=18223

P. 90

Foe interview by AJ Showtime. "Rap Attack." WERQ-FM, October 27, 2024.

Monroe, Rachel. "A Linguist Explains the Baltimore Accent (and Kathy Bates)." Baltimore Fishbowl, October 23, 2014. https://baltimorefishbowl.com/stories/kathy-batess-baltimore-ish-accent/

P. 101

Elkin, Todd. "Scenius, Inspiration, and Invention." Art21, October 25, 2017. https://art21.org/read/scenius-inspiration-and-invention/

P. 103

Shipley, Al. "Class is in Session." Baltimore City Paper, February 18, 2009. http://www2.citypaper.com/music/review.asp?rid=14457

P. 106

Shipley, Al. "The Best of Both Worlds." Baltimore City Paper, July 19, 2006. https://web.archive.org/web/20060721093922/http://www.citypaper.com/special/story.asp?id=12048

P. 108

DJ Booman interview by Chin-Yer Wright. "The Baltimore Scene." WEAA-FM, June 7, 2024.

"Bernie Rabinowitz, 60, founded chain of record stores." The Baltimore Sun, January 23, 2003.
https://www.baltimoresun.com/2003/01/23/bernie-rabinowitz-60-founded-chain-of-record-stores/

P. 117
Shipley, Al. "What the Game's Been Missing: The Return of Tim Trees." Baltimore City Paper, December 7, 2005.
https://web.archive.org/web/20060627112848/http://www.citypaper.com/music/story.asp?id=11199

P. 120
Shipley, Al. "Bossman returns to 'Land of the O' to throw first pitch for Orioles." The Baltimore Banner, August 23, 2023.
https://web.archive.org/web/20240302134439/https://www.thebaltimorebanner.com/culture/music/bossman-orioles-first-pitch-land-of-the-o-O3KKRKBDZBBU5AVJ7BZICCGYQA/

P. 122
"Pharrell Louis Vuitton Baltimore Club." YouTube video, April 5, 2007.
https://www.youtube.com/watch?v=fvIiBmE5A-g

Rodriguez, Jayson and Shaheem Reid. "Mixtape Monday: Kanye West Glows in the Dark; Pharrell Brings the B-More Beats." MTV News, May 21, 2007.
http://www.mtv.com/bands/m/mixtape_monday/052107/

P. 124

"K-Swift's lasting impact." The Baltimore Sun, July 26, 2011.
https://www.baltimoresun.com/2011/07/26/k-swifts-lasting-impact/

"DJ K-Swift making her debut at Twilight Zone in Baltimore, MD 1997." YouTube video, 2016.
https://www.youtube.com/watch?v=koXN9sKLLnY

P. 125

Shipley, Al. "The Club Beat Remembers DJ K-Swift With Club Queen Entertainment." Baltimore City Paper, August 6, 2008.
https://web.archive.org/web/20080809140152/http://www.citypaper.com/digest.asp?id=16118

P. 126

Shipley, Al. "Khia 'DJ K-Swift' Edgerton, Oct. 19, 1978 – July 21, 2008." Baltimore City Paper, July 30, 2008.
https://web.archive.org/web/20110722071838/http://www2.citypaper.com/music/review.asp?rid=13668

P. 129

Shipley, Al. "Blaq is Back." Baltimore City Paper, December 18, 2013.
https://web.archive.org/web/20131219102814/http://citypaper.com/music/blaq-is-back-1.1602324

P. 132

Shipley, Al. "The Club Beat with DJ Mic Marvelous." Baltimore City Paper, November 30, 2007.

http://www.citypaper.com/digest.asp?id=14906

P. 135

Shipley, Al. "The Club Beat with Dukeyman." Baltimore City Paper, April 18, 2008.

https://web.archive.org/web/20080624234302/http://www.citypaper.com/digest.asp?id=15605

P. 144

Seward, Scott. "Why Baltimore House Music is the New Dylan." Post Road Magazine, 2003.

https://www.postroadmag.com/2020/07/23/issue-03/

P. 147

Seward, Scott. "Do Dew the Crabtown Clam." The Village Voice, April 8, 2003.

https://www.villagevoice.com/do-dew-the-crabtown-clam/

P. 153

Fernando, S.H. "Dance the Pain Away." Spin, December 3, 2005.

https://www.spin.com/2005/12/dance-pain-away/

P. 156

Janis, Stephen. "Labtekwon & Rod Lee Interview." Link: A Critical Journal on the Arts, 2005.

P. 157

"Breaking Out." The Baltimore Sun, August 21, 2005. https://www.baltimoresun.com/2005/08/21/breaking-out-5/

P. 160

Harvell, Jess. "On The Corner." Baltimore City Paper, August 30, 2006. https://web.archive.org/web/20071218092514/http://www.citypaper.com/music/story.asp?id=12203

P. 164

Shipley, Al. "The Club Beat with King Tutt." Baltimore City Paper, October 19, 2007. https://web.archive.org/web/20071021063241/http://www.citypaper.com/digest.asp?id=14674

P. 166

Embert, Casey. "HEY GRIFF!: Baltimore club icon steps away from 92Q's 9 o'clock mix." The Baltimore Sun, February 24, 2017. https://www.baltimoresun.com/2017/02/24/hey-griff-baltimore-club-icon-steps-away-from-92qs-9-oclock-mix/

P. 171
Shipley, Al. "The Club Beat with DJ Tigga." Baltimore City Paper, August 31, 2007.
https://web.archive.org/web/20071012074310/http://www.citypaper.com/digest.asp?id=14041

P. 172
Shipley, Al. "The Club Beat with Jonny Blaze." Baltimore City Paper, July 24, 2009.
https://web.archive.org/web/20090727212245/http://www.citypaper.com/digest.asp?id=18403

P. 177
Shipley, Al. "Gettin' Theirs." Baltimore City Paper, June 21, 2006.
https://web.archive.org/web/20070220002431/http://www.citypaper.com/music/review.asp?rid=10470

P. 179
Shipley, Al. "Represent the World Town." Urbanite, July 2, 2012.
https://web.archive.org/web/20120927215357/http://www.urbanitebaltimore.com/baltimore/represent-the-world-town/Content?oid=1474904

P. 189

Shipley, Al. "The Club Beat with Shawn Caesar." Baltimore City Paper, December 19, 2008. http://www.citypaper.com/digest.asp?id=17157

Shipley, Al. "The Club Beat with DJ Chris J." Baltimore City Paper, September 21, 2007. https://web.archive.org/web/20071012004842/http://www.citypaper.com/digest.asp?id=14554

P. 190

Shipley, Al. "The Club Beat with DJ Frie." Baltimore City Paper, November 7, 2008. https://web.archive.org/web/20100218104721/http://www.citypaper.com/digest.asp?id=17003

P. 197

"XLR8R's Best of 2013." XLR8R, December 17, 2012. https://xlr8r.com/features/xlr8r-s-best-of-2012-tracks-part-one/

P. 202

Hogan, Marc. "Hear Blaqstarr's Breezy 'She Is Love.'" Spin, April 30, 2012. https://www.spin.com/2012/04/hear-blaqstarrs-breezy-she-love/

P. 203

Burney, Lawrence. "A Brief History of the Club Music You're Hearing Drake Attempt on Honestly, Nevermind." Vulture, June 19, 2022.
https://www.vulture.com/2022/06/drake-honestly-nevermind-club-music-influences.html

P. 205

Shipley, Al. "Meet Tate Kobang, the East Baltimore Guy Who Flipped a Hometown Classic into a Label Deal." The Fader, August 17, 2015.
https://www.thefader.com/2015/08/17/tate-kobang-bank-rolls

P. 206

Al Shipley. "Tate Kobang: Walking in the Clouds." Pigeons and Planes, April 12, 2016.
https://www.complex.com/pigeons-and-planes/a/pigeons/tate-kobang-baltimore-walking-cloud

P. 211

"Street Sign Revealed for Jimmy Jones, Baltimore Club Music Legend." WJZ News, July 23, 2021.
https://www.cbsnews.com/baltimore/news/street-sign-revealed-for-jimmy-jones-baltimore-club-music-legend-on-the-street-he-grew-up-on/

P. 213

Shipley, Al. "DDm Came Up in Baltimore's Macho Battle-Rap Scene. Then He Came Out." Bandwidth, August 1, 2014.
http://bandwidth.wamu.org/a-former-battle-rap-champ-ddm-hits-the-reset-button-on-himself/

REPEATER BOOKS

is dedicated to the creation of a new reality. The landscape of twenty-first-century arts and letters is faded and inert, riven by fashionable cynicism, egotistical self-reference and a nostalgia for the recent past. Repeater intends to add its voice to those movements that wish to enter history and assert control over its currents, gathering together scattered and isolated voices with those who have already called for an escape from Capitalist Realism. Our desire is to publish in every sphere and genre, combining vigorous dissent and a pragmatic willingness to succeed where messianic abstraction and quiescent co-option have stalled: abstention is not an option: we are alive and we don't agree.